To: A

Miss you.
God Bless
Bob Kaminski

Lying Wonders

Evil Encounters
of a Close Kind

by Bob Kaminski

WinePress Publishing **WP** *Mukilteo, WA 98275*

Contents

PART ONE
THE LUCIFERIC INITIATION

PART TWO
UFO/ALIEN INVOLVEMENT

PART THREE
CREDIBILITY AND NEW AGE RELIGION

Foreword

The UFO phenomenon—what does it mean to the Church of Jesus Christ? How would we Bible-believing, Bible-preaching Christians respond if alien beings from other planets and galaxies suddenly landed and met with the U.S. President on the White House lawn? Would "believers" in Jesus have their faith so shaken that they would turn away and follow the New Age agenda? I believe many would.

In recent years the overwhelming popularity of UFOs, and the actual desire to have a personal "close encounter" has skyrocketed amongst people in the western world. Statistical reports of aliens abducting humans are on the increase, and it has become fashionable to believe in aliens. Through the various modern mediums of communication, aliens and UFOology have come into vogue. In the shopping malls everywhere you can find alien faces, names and symbols on skateboards, roller skates, games, and even clothing lines promoting their realism. Hollywood has not been idle either. Movies such as *"Close Encounters," "Communion," "Enemy Mine," "Star Trek," "Star Wars"* etc., have all served to bring us closer to accepting the possibility of life on other planets—and the "hope" that we will finally come face-to-face with beings from some far off galaxy. But if there is life on other planets, what does this do to our theology?

I was raised in a Christian pastor's home, and imbedded in my upbringing were all the Biblical truths and well-known Bible stories. However, I slipped away to accept the lies of the anti-christ cults that abounded in the '60s and '70s. Even though I had a Christian upbringing, I had never converted my life to submit and surrender to serve the Living God—Jesus Christ. I had never dedicated my life to believing in, and serving only Jesus Christ...I sought to be a god of my own making. I was swept away with the New Age promises of reaching higher levels of consciousness by practicing a certain "tried and proven" system and discipline. These systems all turned out to be demonically inspired.

In the early '70s I was on a search for *the* meaning to my life, and became an active participant in a number of New Age ideas and disciplines. From L. Ron Hubbard's Scientology, to Transcendental Mediation, LSD experiences, and The Great White Brotherhood with it's ascended masters, I did nearly every form of new age belief that I could find. By the grace of God I was delivered from them all by the Lord Jesus, and brought into His saving grace in 1986.

However, being Born Again did not erase the reality of the New Age agenda. Even though I have been cleansed and delivered from the occultic new age religions I must remind myself that they still remain a real threat to those who are unaware of their dangers. I hope this book will somehow serve to be an alert to those souls who are trapped by the end times evil that prevails around us.

In this book, author Robert Kaminski presents a windfall of vital information concerning alien beings, UFOs, subtle New Age indoctrinations. It is information that today's Church needs to read and digest in order to properly prepare us for the soon-to-come end times. As a writer, he articulates with clarity, and has the big picture. In *"Lying Wonders: Evil Encounters of a Close Kind"* he addresses his subject in down-to-earth, practical ways. Read it, study it, and may you be powerfully blessed.

Chuck Dean

Introduction

Society is being moved dramatically toward a more exciting and vibrant existence, with the potential of experiencing power displays offered through a planetary consciousness. The scientific community has usually ignored anything spiritual, related to religion, or para psychology experiences. However, a new breed of Scientist has appeared on the scene. Scientists who are now tapping into a spiritual consciousness, looking for knowledge and meaning to life through psychic experiences, and an opportunity to vibrate together. I believe these scientists, led by their psychic awareness experiences, have a common theme in the Luciferic Initiation. An initiation, which is poisoning the mind and spirit of a large segment of society.

This book will explain, in a practical way, the meaning of the Luciferic Initiation, and tie it together with strange occultic and para-normal events now becoming common-place in society.

While trying to define it, a pastor friend of mine, once said, "the *Luciferic Initiation* may be as simple as getting people to accept demons into their lives." That is exactly what I believe is happening. People are accepting demonic influence as personal guidance, as I will demonstrate in the body of this book.

1

A Foundation of Rebellion

There is nothing new about the New Age movement. Each generation and era adds a slightly new twist to the same old tricks Satan has always employed. The New Age for Adam and Eve began when Satan first interpreted what God said in the Garden of Eden. Satan is again explaining to mankind the benefits of his interpretation in our day. It is called the New Age movement.

This movement, has gained popularity and strength in recent years and is also referred to as the "self-help" movement. Its roots go back as far as ancient paganism—to 19th-century spiritism and the counterculture of the 1960's, when the flower children rejected materialism in favor of *eastern mysticism. Other elements associated with the New Age include: *occultic experiences, *inner transformation, *chanting, *reincarnation, *extraterrestrial beings, *shamanism, *psychic healing, *astral travel, and even *inner healing that many Christian "counselors" are in to.

Many Christian writers have covered the dangers of the New Age movement. For example, Constance

Cumbey, wrote the book, "*Hidden Dangers of the Rainbow*," on the subject. Tal Brooke, author of "*When The World Will Be As One*," and Johanna Michaelson, who wrote "*The Beautiful Side of Evil*," are two more. In 1990, John Anderson, (a former psychic and New Age guru), produced and released a video program by Lighthouse Productions exposing New Age thinking, which is entitled, "*The Lucifer Connection*." The video graphically shows how occult practices of the New Age are being mixed with traditional Christianity. If these people are accurate in their assessments, there appears to be a real threat to the Christian Church.

A merging of science and spirituality is now providing the building blocks for a new religion. It is based on knowledge plus a faith in some kind of an unknown. The unknown, however, is what makes this approach a threat to traditional religion. Instead of one God, as in Christianity, it embraces ancient myth, folklore and stories of many gods and goddesses. The God of the Bible becomes obliterated in the explanations and understanding of complex theories about chaos, order and disorder.

In the October 1994 issue of *Omni* Magazine, Ralph Abraham, who is a prominent mathematician, delves into this ether zone. He indicates renewal of religion as being essential for the growth of a vibrant "*planetary culture." He also says, "The old religions don't work...". He mentions that what ever inhibited the religious evolution over the centuries can be pruned away.[1] This kind of thinking, is at the very core of what I believe will eventually lead to intolerance of traditional Christian values. It is frightening indeed, to realize that even good people with positive intentions are being swept up in the new religion of the mind and psychic experiences.

David Spangler, an influential New Age leader, has indicated that no one will come into the New Age movement without having first gone through the Luciferic Initiation.[2] His comment stirred my curiosity. I began to seriously review what many New Agers have been writing over the last ten years. On the surface, the New Age movement appears harmless. The writers and speakers of the New Age movement seem to mean well. There is no blatant avocation to overthrow the government, or threaten society at large. Peace and tranquillity are preached. There is an emphasis on turning to our inner self, merging ourselves with the cosmos, and giving mother earth the status of a living god. Surely, if we blend these principles and other teachings of "wise men" we should find truth. Right?...Wrong!

The New Age movement, including all its positive aspects, has become a corrupting influence on society, leading many to look for psychic experiences and fulfillment in things that are forbidden by the Bible.

Slowly but surely, we are swallowing the poison that is meant to change, transform, and cause society to follow the greatest deceiver who ever existed, Satan himself. As a Christian, I began to question and be concerned about society's rush toward physic endeavors. What I found was a subliminal plan emerging from New Age books and articles. The plan appears enticing, but I believe elements of the plan are demonic in nature— I believe that a Satanic plan was formulated. It is evidenced in many books like Whitley Strieber's best sellers about UFO/alien visitations.

After fourteen years of being a charismatic Christian and a lay minister, I sensed a real threat from these New Age teachings, and their emphasis on the occult and humanism. It appeared that these teachings were a veiled replacement for God.

The saying, "man can do anything he puts his mind to," is admirable and widely accepted. We are taught this at an early age. Hard work in school and at our jobs is certainly acceptable, normal rewardable behavior. However, the New Age teachings go beyond this. It elevates our human capacities to say, "man can solve most of his social problems while rising at the same time to a new spiritual consciousness.

It is not surprising that society seems to be embracing more of these teachings, but it is startling to see a large segment of the Christian church falling into the ambush of this same pattern of thinking. I believe this to be a trap, leading the church away from basic Biblical precepts. New Age teaching implies that humanism is good and the old Biblical taboos, such as witchcraft and channeling (talking with the dead) are not at all bad. It implies, that man's mind over matter (a technique of *holistic medicine), for example, is also the new wave of healing. It also implies that we are all potentially gods. However, it is okay even for a "god" to have an "ancient spirit" guide to help along the way towards transcending our physical bodies.

Of course, not all churches embrace this deception, but many have accepted one or more New Age principles as part of their faith/belief system. Humanism together with, "*Values Clarification," "*Situational Ethics," and in some cases *Shamanism and the occult have crept into the church scene. One could say, "no society is perfect and no church is perfect," though this is just an excuse to do anything we want in the name of experiment, knowledge, and education. God warned us about dabbling in the occult, as well as the consequences if we ignore His warning.

The path to the Luciferic Initiation is clear from the established works of both Christian and New Age writers. In the book, *UFO's in the New Age*, author William M. Alnor mentions some of the writings of David Spangler concerning the Luciferic Initiation. He says:

"David Spangler, one of the world's most influential New Age leaders who claims to be in touch with a variety of entities, (including aliens) states that we must be initiated into Lucifer in order to enter the New Age."[3]

He further quotes Spangler, writing:

"Lucifer comes to give to us the final gift of wholeness. If we accept it (*the gift*) then he (*Satan*) is free and we are free. That is the Luciferic Initiation. It is one that many people now and in the days ahead will be facing, for it is an initiation into the New Age."[4]

Texe Marrs, the Christian author of "*Mystery Mark of the New Age,*" indicates the devilish importance of the Luciferic Initiation.

He writes, "Paul prophesied in 2 Thessalonians 2, that after the Antichrist has come and declares himself to the world as God, the vast majority will be allowed strong delusion by God. They will believe in this horrid world leader and eventually worship him as God. They will accept his Luciferic Initiation because they first rejected the Truth, which is Christ Jesus..."[5]

Texe Marrs further indicates how the initiation will be accomplished. His idea suggests that the mark of the beast which is planned for everyone, is also tied to the Luciferic Initiation.

"New Age citizens will not have to worry about how they are going to get to the churches, synagogues, and temples to be initiated and given the Mark. In the New Age, an individual's salvation is considered to be an outmoded Christian concept. *Universal love, unity, and group consciousness are the ideals for the New Age..."[6] Texe Marrs quotes the New Age leader, Benjamin Creme about the group formation initiation.

"We are entering the 'crisis of Love.' This is the experience which the human race faces as it enters that period when it will, as a whole.....take place in the *Kingdom of Souls. During the *Aquarian Age, the aim of the Christ, *Maitreya, the *Hierophant at the first two initiations, will be to initiate millions of people in group formation into the *Hierarchy.... Vast numbers will take the first and some will take the second initiation. This is an extraordinary event to be happening on a mass scale. It shows the success of the evolutionary plan as it is envisaged by the Lord of the World, *Sanat Kumara, or *Shamballa, and carried out by his agents the *Planetary Hierarchy."[7]

Benjamin Creme, may be right when it comes to the mass initiations, but I differ with him on the number of events. I believe the Luciferic Initiation is already being implemented (as indicated by Spangler), and not with any consistent visible mark. Events surrounding many incidents of UFOs and alien visitations, suggest that people are already being programmed and modified (initiated), to become the future leaders of this *mass initiation. In later chapters, I will discuss why I believe the Luciferic Initiation is a current, ongoing event.

So as Christian saints, are we to sit by idly as Christian's have done so often in the past, and wait for "someone else" to take the initiative in exposing this very real threat to society? Perhaps after reading this book, you will be *the* someone, who will take the initiative; at least in your corner of the world. If nothing else, it will spur some to seriously question these strange occurring events which range from occult experiences to UFO's and crop circles. Humanism and *moral relativism, that sound so good on the surface, carry with them a multitude of dilemmas. We must be alerted to this.

First, humanistic standards are always shifting. The abortion movement is a classic example of this. Pregnancy, seen as an uncomfortable inconvenience, is used to justify abortion from a humanistic point of view.

Our society finds itself in a continuing predicament over issues such as, feminism, education, divorce, alternative civil rights causes, violence, and in particular— youth violence.

While considering where many of these liberal thinking people came from, I realized they are leftovers from the table of the "*Aquarian Age." Remember the flower children of the late sixties and early seventies who bloomed about the time God was pronounced dead? When God is left behind, a replacement is usually sought out. The counterculture society of the 1960's began with rebellion against parents, followed with rebellion against all forms of authority. In large part the youth of that era rebelled against the constraints of traditional and moral values, using the Vietnam war as a spearhead. They roamed the country looking for the perfect carefree life, with free love, a Volkswagen bus, and a dog named Boo. The replacement for God? Marijuana, some LSD and eastern mysticism chants (or loud rock and roll music) were all they needed for a trip to Nirvana.

This aimless youth movement was no more obvious than in California, where I lived in the early 1970's. A trip down the coastal highway 101 (in Santa Barbara) yielded a harvest of shoulder to shoulder hitchhikers, all young, some with children and dogs all going somewhere but nowhere in particular. Looking back, I believe this wave of rebellion was a significant event, planned and executed straight from the office of Hell. It did exactly what it was meant to do. It fostered rebellion, opened the door to increased drug use and promoted deterioration of moral values. That rebellion was a *"set up"* for creating a future moral relativistic society, which we suffer from today.

The after shock of that rebellion is now coming into full view as part of the overall New Age encroachment. The assault on authority and the breakdown of the family unit has passed over our society like a gigantic wave leaving many young people looking for some kind of fulfillment. The hippies of the sixties may have grown up, but something poisonous remained in their attitudes, and passed on to their children. These are the same people who have entered into mainstream societies, setting the agendas for government, schools, and mainline churches (See Figure 1). They hold government positions, teach, and are influential members of the media.

I sat down one night and tried to create a list of functions in society that we embrace as part of our normal lifestyle. In reality, these functions prepare us for the advancement of the Luciferic Initiation.

I began listing items (which include mindsets, etc.) in society that are accepted as, "in" or "normal." These are items that traditional Christianity did not previously accept or embrace. This process forced me to look into many unusual subjects, some with New Age origin. What I discovered is evidence that Satan's plan for the

Luciferic Initiation was slowly being implemented all along. I became overwhelmed at the increasing exposure to strange things like flying saucers, aliens, animal mutilations, and *crop circles. With frequent but sporadic media coverage, it can be seen that society is beginning to view these as everyday events. A few years ago they were practically unknown. Also on the increase is our preoccupation with psychic events, *parapsychology, *hauntings, and so forth. Not long ago these events were viewed suspiciously as evil. Now, they have become common place and are mainstream entertainment events.

I believe there is a definite correlation between all of these supernatural events and the New Age movement, which is Satan's plan to draw as many people as possible away from the true and living God of the Bible. New Age ideas and activities are tools Satan uses to draw unsuspecting people into his "initiation web." They are all part of the ultra deceptive *"Lying Wonders"* now being levied upon mankind.

Being a graduate engineer who analyzes everything at one time, I was not a believer in UFO's. But now I believe they are one of the lying wonders which have appeared in the heavens for centuries. My belief in the existence of UFOs is based on a factual incident. The "Roswell, New Mexico incident," which took place in 1947, has been covered at great length on several television programs and many written accounts. Featured writers, witnesses and stories about the event started me re-thinking the issue of flying saucers.

Books like, *"UFO Crash at Roswell," "Out There,"* and *"Above Top Secret,"* and many others suggest there was a major cover-up by the US Government concerning a crashed flying saucer in the desert near Roswell, New

Mexico. These books strongly suggest that the physical evidence, including alien bodies found nearby, were confiscated by the US Army. Why would I believe it? Because I believe the credibility of many of the witnesses, who finally spoke out after being coerced into silence for so many years. They had nothing to gain but scorn, yet they told their stories convincingly and without any apparent self motive. (*Note*: Even though demons cannot die as we know death...the bodies that they were using, disguised as aliens from another world, did die in this crash.)

If just ten percent of the facts reported in books like "*UFO Crash at Roswell*" and "*Above Top Secret*" are reliable, we as Christians have to re-access our position concerning these events. We can either ignore what is fast becoming obvious to many UFO researchers, or we can evaluate these strange events according to God's Word.

Spiritual matters are not easily understood or accurately examined by the material or secular world. So it is up to the Christian body, through Godly discernment, to assess if the UFO "event" is of God or not. There is no in between solution. To believe otherwise would open the door to many deceptions. Witnesses like the New Mexico rancher Mac Brazel, who found the downed UFO and Major Jesse A. Marcel, as well as others involved in the Roswell incident indicated hard evidence did exist. Their personal involvement convinced me that saucers and their alien contents are real.

In later chapters, I will explore what I believe UFO's are, their purpose and their part in the Luciferic Initiation, currently being projected on mankind.

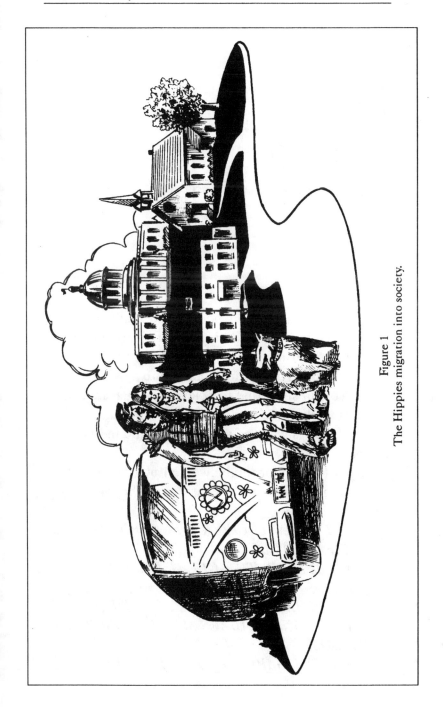

Figure 1
The Hippies migration into society.

2

What is the Luciferic Initiation?

Churches and society are being invaded and reshaped by New Age ideologies. This invasion, is usually experienced through an initiation called "The Luciferic Initiation". Though not clearly apparent to most, this is an invasion of our spirit due to a clever spiritual adversary, who is at work in the world undermining mankind. Lucifer, or Satan is working to bring mankind in line with his goals.

My definition for the New Age Luciferic Initiation slowly comes into focus by considering the following:

1. *THE TERM LUCIFERIC IS DERIVED FROM LUCIFER/SATAN*
2. *LUCIFER IS THE GREAT DECEIVER AND LIAR*
3. *SATAN HAS A PLAN TO DECEIVE THE WORLD*
4. *HIS PLAN REQUIRES MAN TO ACCEPT HIS WISDOM*
5. *HIS EMISSARIES PROMOTE HIS PLAN*

6. *HE MUST PREPARE MAN TO ACCEPT HIS PLAN*

7. *HE MUST FIND A WAY TO INVADE THE SPIRIT TO PUT HIS PLAN INTO ACTION*

8. *HIS PLAN THEN IS TO USE THESE VOLUNTEERS TO FIGHT GOD AND HIS FOLLOWERS*

These statements are not new to many Christians. Though to the "lukewarm" and to the unbeliever they appear as foolishness; or ideas leading to another conspiracy theory perhaps. Who would believe in such a ridiculous idea?

The attitude of unbelief is precisely what makes the whole idea so possible. The unbeliever, who sees things only from their own intellectual point of view, easily becomes manipulated by Satan and his willing volunteers. The matter of the Luciferic Initiation, is so important, that we must look honestly and sufficiently into it and its consequences, before we dismiss it.

Humanists quickly portray the Christian as small minded and bigoted. Of course, the assumption is that humanists are not bigoted, just objective and open minded. New Agers (same as "humanists") are often offended when someone dares to come from God's point of view, using His written Word. It simply becomes offensive to offer the mere idea they may might be wrong, deluded and in serious error.

By reviewing the brief list of eight statements noted previously, I have arrived at the definition for the Luciferic Initiation:

A REAL SPIRITUAL CONSCIOUSNESS EVENT WHERE A PERSON ACCEPTS AND EMBRACES UNGODLY WISDOM/ACTIVITY (OFTEN IN IGNO-

*RANCE) IN SUCH A WAY THAT IT GUIDES THEIR
PERSONAL LIFE AND CONVICTIONS.*

The Luciferic activity begins by embracing teachings, like white witchcraft, astrology, or "channeling."
On the surface these teachings seem desirable and may
not be recognized as evil in origin. The result will always be to contradict or misuse God and His Word. It
will cause man to rise to new heights, explaining new
revelations and experiences that make God's teachings
old and out of date. By consciously replacing God and
His teachings, man, in essence, makes himself a god.

Let's examine the Luciferic Initiation a little more
closely now that we have attempted to define it.

The Luciferic Initiation is not something that most
people walk into readily. The vast majority of people do
not want to accept Satan into their lives. Given the informed choice, they just know better.

The initiation "experience" occurs after going
through a series of preparations that appear to be non
threatening, non demonic, non lethal. In fact, it may
offer personal enhancement such as psychic abilities.
The key phrase here is, "appears to be." The master of
deception has not changed. He is still looking for ways
to fool you and me. Unfortunately, he has been successful in making things *appear* acceptable. In reality,
these things are seeds of destruction being planted in
the field where you and I grow. His plan of deception
simply would not work if it were easy for man to figure
out and see it for what it is. Ultimately, Satan's plan for
the unwary is to get them to join him in the fight against
God and suffer his fate of eternal judgment.

Satan does this so as to get a person to believe in
something not directly connected to demons, hell or

himself. This is why the advent of UFOs, aliens, angels, demonic miracles and psychic displays are so important to his plan. All these things raise man to a higher consciousness level and a pseudo heaven.

New Age Demonic Activity

When referring to demonic activity, most of us think of someone acting very weird, foaming at the mouth, shouting profanity, and definitely not under their own control. Usually, they look, act and sound like someone other than themselves. Their conduct may seem threatening to themselves and to others, perhaps, even showing signs of epilepsy. You may be reminded of the movie, *The Exorcist*, if you were unfortunate enough to have seen it. This is a common description of someone possessed or demonic.

Based on the Word of God (the Holy Bible), this type of activity is Satanic in origin, and the Christian world has accurately labeled this phenomena as demonic. However, for the purpose of this book, I intend to deal with another type of demonic activity. One that is so insidious, that it can deceive those who do not act possessed in the traditional sense. Instead, they look and act normal, are intelligent, but have been infused with demonic wisdom and carry out this evil wisdom in a seemingly reasonable way. I am reminded of a Biblical saying that reads, *"there is a way that seems right to a man, but the end thereof is death"*[1]—this is a real and spiritual death!

The wisdom of the New Age era is really nothing more than a new twist of Satan's old lie that has been around since the fall of Adam. Paul, the Apostle, spoke about this in the Book of Ephesians, Chapter 6, Verse

12, as evil power from on high. It has never been fulfilling and never will be. Yet, many try to promote the New Age mentality as fresh and better than anything anyone has ever devised. Have you ever wondered why there are so many so-called, "old masters?" If just one of them really had ALL the answers to life, would it not boil down to only one "old master?" Satan's old ideas are being re-packaged to look new to today's discoverer. However, let us be reminded of a section from the Book of Ecclesiastes, "there is nothing new under the sun."[2] There are no new revelations from God waiting to be discovered. There are only new people rediscovering old ideas from the "ancient ones" (evil powers on high, or human gurus), setting man all up for another fall.

Enticements used to ensnare interested new comers are generally offered through psychic abilities like communicating with guides (demons) through channeling, and spiritual exercises given through so-called enlightenment seminars. These psychic enhancements, along with other supernatural phenomena, are meant to provide a person some special ability they didn't previously have.

Now that we have tackled the definition and discussed it, we are back to the question, "What is the Luciferic Initiation"? *It is simply Satan's spiritual technique to mislead and deceive people of this world through a planetary spiritual consciousness and demonic wisdom to believe something other than the truth of God's Word.*

In his book, *"To Hell and Back,"* Maurice S. Rawlings M.D. mentions the Luciferic Initiation. He described various near death experiences (NDE) and out of body experiences (OBE) some people had in trauma (emergency) situations. While he personally observed trauma and critical medical situations over many years, several incidents stood out as bizarre with unexplainable spiritual connotations. Not understanding the strange antics these people were going through, he began to research Christian and non-Christian materials, hoping to find out what really was happening to these trauma victims. What he found, was a definite connection with some of these experiences and the existence of a real hell. Others had very pleasant experiences, pointing to the existence of God. While paging through his book, I was astonished to find a reference to the Luciferic Initiation. He describes the "spiritual consciousness event" I mention in my definition of the Luciferic initiation as follows:

"*Shakti-pat is yet another synonym for the force which super guru *Baba Muktananda uses to baptize his followers. When a person receives this force, they fall down in a trance, experiencing instantaneous "enlightenment," introducing them to their "infinite potential," and their "oneness with the universe. This is elsewhere called the "Luciferic initiation" by adherent David Spangler."[3]

Although Doctor Rawlings references a specific *enlightenment* event, I'm certain this is not the only way to become an *initiate. As you will see later on, I believe there are many ways to fall under the New Age Luciferic Control. A few New Age adherents indicate there will be *mass initiations. As I have previously indicated, this may happen, but I believe it is happening now to individuals and small groups.

The direction that society is headed is described in Figure 2-1. Note that as time progresses, the New Age darkness seems to have greater influence. I'm not prepared to say that the items are on a one-to-one direct proportion as shown in Figure 2-1. However, the more societies give up traditional God fearing values, the more they are replaced with New Age values. Another possible way to show this is shown in Figure 2-2.

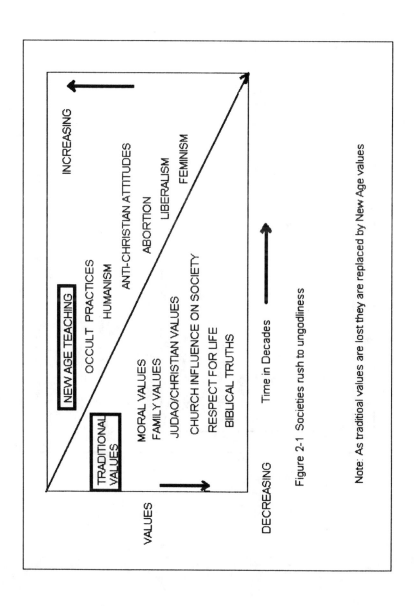

Figure 2-1 Societies rush to ungodliness

Note: As traditional values are lost they are replaced by New Age values

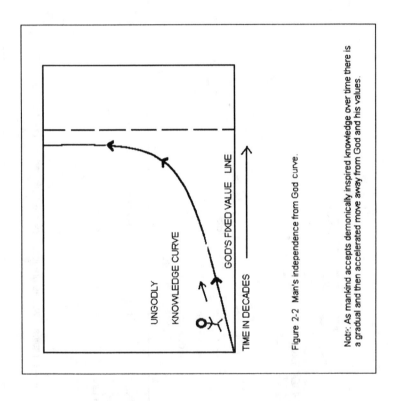

Figure 2-2 Man's independence from God curve.

Note: As mankind accepts demonically inspired knowledge over time there is a gradual and then accelerated move away from God and his values.

3

Purpose of the Luciferic Initiation

The main purpose of the Luciferic Initiation, is to mark or seal a person into Satan's service. It enlists them to follow his wisdom and to carry out his mandate and plan.

Since Satan had some success in thwarting God's plan for mankind (like in the Garden of Eden), he has also set into motion an elaborate plan that enlists mankind in helping him thwart God. Satan and his helpers are busy preparing mankind for this defiance against God, and in the process lay the ground work for our own destruction.

In Isaiah, Chapter 14, 17-21, it appears that the King of Tyre (Satan) has no desire to help man, but to use and consume man in his plan to stop God at any cost. You and I are the cost! He paid his price and it wasn't good enough— Satan gambled and lost. His ultimate fate is eternal punishment for direct rebellion. Since his fall from grace, Satan's plan and purpose has been aimed against God. He has not been successful in a di-

rect approach. As you may remember, he was kicked
out of God's presence (Isaiah 14:12- 15). The only probable option left for him, is to try to afflict God indi-
rectly. This is where you and I fit into his plan, through
the Luciferic Initiation.

Satan's plan is to bring God's creation to shambles.
We are part of God's creation and He said it was good
(Genesis 1:31). The Luciferic Initiation is a specific
method and technique that Satan uses to confuse
people and cause them to think about themselves in
ways that "religion" has inadequately prepared us for,
or warned us about. In Satan's approach, the full emphasis will be on the all important "you," by feeding
the ego. This allows us to put ourselves on the pedestal
of self-importance, which is a form of self-idolatry. The
Bible on the other hand teaches that we are to die to
self, humble ourselves and see the other person as more
important than our self. This is the opposite of what is
taught in the New Age movement—*despite its humanistic
caring*!

The importance of stroking our "I" centered ego
appeals to our greedy appetite for recognition, ability,
money, and fame. You might ask how does the average
person fall into this trap? One way can be through well
intentioned programs that assist a person in their development to get ahead. Many realize, the need for self-
improvement courses in order to become better trained
and educated. This in itself is not the problem. However, education with the wrong focus can be. For instance, the three R's (reading, 'riting, 'rithmetic) rep-
resenting basic education are to enable us to function
in society, hold a job, pay the bills, raise a family, and
perhaps go on to a higher education for acquiring additional skills. Notice the importance of higher educa-

tion today. We send our sons and daughters off to colleges and universities with the hope of helping them to excel in today's world. This again is not wrong, but what they receive can be highly questionable depending on the teacher's personal agenda and course content.

The fount of knowledge that most of us drink from has become diluted and polluted. It has become enlarged with diverse philosophies, courses and information that are morally questionable. The old adage, "knowledge can never hurt you," seems to justify the idea that it is okay to fill your head with nonsense courses and data you may (or may not) conceivably need someday. This "innocent" approach to all knowledge is exactly what I believe Satan wants. He desires society to accept the idea that it is reasonable to pursue knowledge of any kind, without constraints. This idea amounts to establishing a right to eat the fruit from the tree of knowledge of good and evil, originally found in the Garden of Eden. This is exactly what most of us have done.

After being a staunch supporter of the right to all knowledge, I slowly began to see that knowledge of itself, is not the cure-all or key to life as some claim. In fact, knowledge on how to construct a home made bomb, how to commit suicide, alternative life styles, mercy killing, new ways to abort babies, gene splicing of human attributes into animals, and using animal parts in man all came from someone's idea of "enlightened" knowledge. It amounts to a mentality that says if it can be done, then it should be done.

Science in general and genetic engineering specifically has slipped into a morass of questionable social, moral and religious ethics. Further proof of this, can seen in actions by The National Institute of Health in their recommendation to allow federal funding of human-embryo research. This is another example, of science becoming amoral toward life. Human embryos created in the laboratory for scientific experimental purposes raise serious moral questions. Human embryos are looked on as guinea pigs. The pursuit and acquisition of the wrong kind of knowledge can be lethal for the individual and for society. Here we have good intention, but no regard for human life. This line of thinking undermines life and the dignity of life, not to mention man's invasion of God's creator role. Scripture says that with much knowledge comes much grief (Ecclesiastes 1:18). I wonder if God will hold these researchers accountable for their scientific curiosity.

Today, I don't see genetic researchers looking at possible long range problems in the future that genetic engineering can introduce. Today's quick solution, can create long range human genetics problems not easily resolved. The Catholic Church, which has taken a strong moral stand on this issue rejects all human-embryo research.[1] Perhaps medical science should start listening to the time tested moral voice of the ages.

Through our appetite for knowledge and education, people have made themselves vulnerable to teachings that may be demonically inspired. Being ignorant of the New Age agenda, we are continuously maneuvered into beliefs and actions, which are in opposition to God's principles. Most of the people eating the fruit from the tree of knowledge don't realize they have bitten into one of the cleverest schemes ever laid on mankind. It seems that we are always looking for answers to things we don't understand (Acts 17:21). What else is new in human nature?

Ironically, some of the teachings we have become enmeshed in deal with human behavior, such as *Situational Ethics and *Values Clarification where there are no absolutes. Others take on a religious tone with the practice of eastern mysticism, such as *yoga, *martial arts, *astral projection, *meditation exercises, *reincarnation and reciting *demonic mantras. Not taken very seriously only thirty years ago, today they are integrated in mainstream American society. What happened? Did we lose something or obtain some spiritual attribute that we didn't expect? Were we perhaps, "conditioned" over these last thirty years (since the flower children rebellion in the sixties and seventies), for something that only now is being made manifest? Strange apparitions, communication with the dead, and involvement with spiritual forces were not accepted by a large segment of the population until recently. Today, society seems to have a growing, insatiable hunger for these occultic interests.

Teachers greatly affect the minds of all they instruct. A popular educator with a charismatic personality can use a twisted agenda to mislead many people. No one should aspire to the teaching field unless they are truly gifted and committed. Even this should be balanced and supported with Biblical moral values and basic Judeo/Christian understanding. I say this because the Bible strongly indicates that those who teach will be held at a higher accountability level (James 3:1). Teachers are looked up to, and therefore are trusted as being filled with good, wholesome knowledge to share. I think a lot of society's ills can be laid at the foot of a corrupted knowledge foundation—through evil inspired teaching.

Ungodly spiritual activity has found its way into social acceptance. It is veiled under a large group of items in the preparation of the Luciferic encounter. The following chapter describes that comprehensive list of items.

4

Categories and Examples of Pre-Initiation

There are many ways a person can open the door to receive the Luciferic Initiation. Usually involvement in one or more of the activities listed below, is sufficient to start one moving in that direction. A partial list of the various initiation and pre-initiation activities is shown below. These items signify various opportunities Satan utilizes to establish the ground work in moving unsuspecting people toward a new spirituality. A quick look at the list provides a wide variety of enticements for satanic seduction. Most who are caught in this trap are unaware of the dangers; thus people of all walks of life are involved.

A flow chart indicating how a person might move through the Luciferic Initiation is shown in Figure 4-1. Discussion of the figure is covered at the end of this chapter.

CATEGORIES OF PRE-INITIATION

OCCULTIC ACTIVITIES SUCH AS:

WITCHCRAFT (all types)
SATANIC WORSHIP
HIP (rituals and sacrifices)
COVENS
SPIRIT CHANNELING
TRANSCENDENTAL MEDITATION
VISUALIZATION
SEANCES
ASTRAL PROJECTION
ASTROLOGY
TAROT CARDS
PALM READING
TABLE THUMPING
MOVING OBJECTS BY MIND CONTROL
"DUNGEONS AND DRAGONS"/"MAGIC"
DRUG ADDICTION
SUPERSTITIONS
COMMUNICATION WITH THE DEAD
OUIJA BOARD
AUTOMATIC WRITING AND AUTOMATIC ART
PSYCHIC HEALING
HOLISTIC HEALING
TEA LEAF READING
DEMONIC VIDEO GAMES
READING ANIMAL ENTRAILS

RELIGIOUS CULTS:

MORMONISM *
MASONS

SATANIC CHURCHES
GAY CHURCHES
COVENS
NEW AGE CHURCHES
HINDUISM
BUDDHISM *
NATIVE RELIGIONS
BAHAI FAITH *
JEHOVAH WITNESSES
SCIENCE CHURCHES (I.E. Scientology, Science of the Mind, etc.) *
WORLDLY PHILOSOPHIES
(* As defined in Kingdom of the Cults by the late Walter Martin).

TELEVISION AND MOVIES THAT PORTRAY:

PSYCHIC AND SUPERNATURAL THEMES
GLORIFICATION OF CRIME
GRAPHIC VIOLENCE
SEXUAL PROMISCUITY
IMMORAL AND DEVIANT LIFE STYLES
MINDLESS ROBOTIC TYPE HEROES
HUMANISTIC VALUES (amoral values with no right or wrong)
MEGA DOSES OF PROFANITY
ANTI-BIBLICAL AND ANTI-CHRISTIAN PRIN-CIPLES
DEMONIC POSSESSION AS ENTERTAINMENT
SUBLIMINAL ADVERTISING (secretive and sugges-tion oriented)

NEWSPAPERS, BOOKS, AND MAGAZINES THAT FEATURE:

GRAPHIC PICTURES OF SEX AND VIOLENCE
HUMANISTIC ARTICLES (promoting situational ethics)
ALTERNATIVE AND DEVIANT SEX LIFESTYLES
PRO ABORTION ARTICLES OR EDITORIALS
ANTI-JUDEO/CHRISTIAN VALUES
SCANDALOUS AND SENSATIONAL MATERIAL
HOROSCOPES AND PSYCHIC ADVISORS

CHURCHES THAT TEACH FALSE DOCTRINES SUCH AS:

THERE IS NO HELL
EVERYONE IS GOING TO HEAVEN
THERE ARE MANY PATHS TO GOD
GOD'S WORD IS DEFECTIVE AND OUT OF DATE
GOD IS FEMININE (Or God is anti-female. There are also sex gender cults)
SOFT LOVE
NEW AGE TENETS
TRANSCENDENTAL MEDITATION
EARTH IS A LIVING GOD OF WHICH WE ARE PART
THERE ARE OTHER SAVIORS
LOOKING TO SAINTS, RATHER THAN GOD
LIBERATION THEOLOGY

HUMANISM/MAN'S SOLUTIONS WITHOUT GOD:

SOCIAL PROGRAMS such as:

ABORTION AND ABORTION COUNSELING
PLANNED PARENTHOOD
SPECIAL RIGHTS FOR GAYS
PLACING CHILDREN IN GAY HOUSEHOLDS
ERA/NOW FEMINIST MOVEMENT
DOCTOR ASSISTED DEATHS
CLINICS AND DOCTORS READY TO ASSIST IN
ABORTION

SCHOOLS WHOSE POLICY IT IS TO:

PRACTICE NEW AGE MEDITATION
TEACH EASTERN RELIGIONS
FORBID PRAYER
INTIMIDATE PEOPLE WHO HAVE JUDEO
CHRISTIAN VALUES
HAND OUT BIRTH CONTROL DEVICES
TEACH ALTERNATIVE AND DEVIANT LIFE
STYLES
TEACH SEX EDUCATION WITHOUT MORAL
VALUES
TEACH TOLERANCE OF HOMOSEXUAL BEHAV-
IOR (DEVIANCY)
TEACH EVOLUTION AS A PROVEN SCIENCE (It
is still only a theory...not proven)
FORBID THE TEACHING OF CREATIONISM

ART FORMS THAT ARE:

SEXUALLY GRAPHIC
SUGGESTIVE AND IMMORAL
CELEBRATING DEVIANCY
DESECRATION OF RELIGIOUS VALUES

MUSIC:

HARD ROCK CONCERTS PROMOTING VIO-
LENCE
EVIL LYRICS
SATANIC SYMBOLS ASSOCIATED (Pentagrams, bro-
ken crosses, amulets, and crystals.)
ANTISOCIAL LYRICS (Rap lyrics that promote cop
killing, anti-female and racist attitudes.)
SEXUALLY SUGGESTIVE LYRICS AND DANCE
ROUTINES

A SOCIAL JUSTICE SYSTEM:

MAKING GODLIKE DECISIONS (okays abortion)
ALLOWING   EXPERIMENTATION   WITH
ABORTED FETUS TISSUE
GIVING SPECIAL RIGHTS TO GAYS
ALLOWING PLACEMENT OF CHILDREN IN GAY
HOUSEHOLDS
CHALLENGING THE CHURCH'S BELIEF SYS-
TEM
INTERPRETING LAWS PREVENTING DEFINI-
TION OF OBSCENITY

OTHER FORMS OF DECEPTION:

NEO NAZI ACTIVITY
KKK ORGANIZATION
REWRITING OF HISTORY

Candidate initiates who are open to New Age and
other spiritual influences may come from Christian or
non-Christian backgrounds. It is obvious that many have

incorporated one or more of these listed options into their personal lives. Involvement for some may be just simple curiosity. For others, it might be serious study leading to spiritual encounters with the occult. These spiritual experiences (some very frightening) are not from God.

The following are examples from the above categories. I developed them in order to describe how prospective candidates can come under these influences and thus become a spokesman for Lucifer. From these examples the reader can develop others as an exercise.

EXAMPLE ONE FROM THE OCCULTIC ACTIVITIES LIST

SPIRIT CHANNELING

People are naturally inquisitive about something mysterious and unknown. Most people usually want to find out what the truth might be regarding a particular mystery. This simple curiosity can become a person's spiritual downfall. Knowledge about some matters spiritually may lead an individual into communication with demons and the associated consequences. For example, communication with demons through seances, can be dangerous and life threatening. God, warned against witchcraft. Still many ignore the warning and run the risk of serious life long demonic encounters.

A person desiring to know about spirit guides and channeling can take one of two roads: 1) Anticipating the journey will eventually lead to evil consequences a person could simply refuse to go any further. 2) Participate further by seeking knowledge where channeling is taught and eventually experience the presence of these so-called guides.

Once a person communicates their desire (to the unseen spirit world) by an act of their will, demons have the right to access that person. They have their authority to influence and eventually control them. At the onset, this is done by seemingly innocent spirit guide visits, (by thought or by visual images), and with the confirming revelation of some apparent, "beneficial" message. The message might be a personal reassurance, that the person is indeed on the right track or that their deceased loved ones are all right and happy. Once contact becomes repetitive, a firm spiritual connection is established and that person becomes a channel for the demon guide. As this occurs, the Luciferic Initiation can begin in earnest. The channel spirit begins to gain greater control by imparting their insights, (like humanistic values), and\or introduces other stronger spirit guides. This takeover sometimes produces statements from demons that make no sense and is confusing. Channeling can be terrifying and not without risk!

As a person continues to open their mind and receive Guide influence, it cannot be easily terminated. From this point on, the demonic activity rapidly increases, teaching and espousing ungodly wisdom that will lead the victim in a direction away from God. This may not initially be apparent to the individual. The demonic activity will ultimately reveal itself to be godless, teaching evil as good, and embracing a false religious spirituality. An example of this might be when a person is told to say a prayer over and over for hours or perhaps claim they had past lives.

So-called channelers are simply people who allow their mind and body to be used by other spiritual forces (demons). They do not always understand these forces to be demons. Their presence usually become known through voice and body language unlike that of the host person. The entity may indicate that it is an ancient spirit and have a name such as "Old Indian Joe". Some channelers see frightening dreams and visions of future world events and still others see signs and wonders in the heavens like flying saucers, apparitions, or aliens.

New Agers who have written books on this subject, often describe awful events dealing with near occasions of madness and debilitating fear when occultic events take place. It's surprising that when so many face the obvious scare of their lives, they continue to believe something other than the truth.

Eventually (unless renounced) the participant becomes a sold out believer just for the use of an occultic gift. Some have said their occultic gift is from God because that idea shields their conscience from the terrifying reality, that it might be from Satan. The psychic gift is not comparable to any of the gifts bestowed by God as mentioned in the Bible. It usually explains a strange wisdom or a new revelation from so-called heavenly beings *(helpers* or *watchers)*.

When a Christian is under the influence of the Holy Spirit, the person is never taken over forcibly. The Holy Spirit always works together and in concert with the conscious believer. This is an important point. God's method is never to force a person against their will. He gave each person free will and He respects that free will, in spite of possible rejection. On the other hand, Satan wishes to control and re-mold a person into his image of dark wisdom and evil if they are willing to channel (connect) with him and his demons.

EXAMPLE TWO FROM THE OCCULTIC ACTIVITY LIST

DUNGEONS AND DRAGONS

Many young people have fallen into the entertainment game trap. Games are fun but there have been stories about persons that have fallen under the power of this game and have entered into a strange fantasy to the point of becoming possessed. Persons may ask, why all the fuss about a game? After all, isn't it just a game? Well meaning people may argue, that the game is not meant to hurt anyone. Good intention however, does not replace the dangers of not being informed. Society in general may not realize the spiritual dangers of a particular game. Perhaps they may not even care that a real, spiritual danger may be poised to harm naive players.

Dungeons and Dragons (D&D) is set up to for a person to learn character role playing, accept power, and do things that will give them more power. This includes killing, casting spells, and playing with demon type characters.

To a bright, impressionable young mind, this game could alter their personality and cause them to come under demonic influence. Those who become involved in the game's role playing aspects, for the purpose of gaining more power, can enter into a long term fantasy becoming candidates that enter into the Luciferic Initiation. The influence of this game, like most other occultic activities, is dependent on how serious the participating individual becomes. None of its influence is good, but the degree of involvement corresponds to the amount of demonic activity which can be found in the player's life.

I believe D&D is an example of a typical precursor, to the Luciferic Initiation. It prepares one to accept ungodly thinking. Desire for power, consulting witches, slaying dragons, casting spells, and killing weird animals and monsters certainly doesn't sound like a training course in good social attitudes and behavior. Instead, it puts the participants on a power trip and leads them to accept non-Christian values and practices. Every now and then, you hear of a sad case where a youth deeply involved in this game has gone berserk and became deadly violent. At some point, make believe became real for him. I don't believe this is a game I believe it is a demonic training session for innocent minds. Surely a trap we need to be warned about.

Other similar games now on video machines have also become popular with the young crowd. These games are meant to be entertainment, but should be avoided. They present an opportunity for the demons to play with us.

EXAMPLE THREE FROM THE OCCULTIC ACTIVITY LIST

OUIJA BOARD

Another deceptive, innocent looking game is the Ouija Board found in most toy stores. This one doesn't appear to be as bad because there are no complex rules, as in D & D. But the mere willingness to play this game telegraphs to unseen powers a person's vulnerability for adventure and experiment. The spiritual world will network with anyone showing an interest in this game as a means of entrapment.

As the player(s) run their hand over the Ouija board with the game slider, the person(s) is mentally summoning an invisible power to come and make its presence known. The invisible entity will answer questions about many subjects including the future or advice on pending decisions. The unseen intelligence, responds by spelling out the answer with the letters of the alphabet that appear on the board. This activity is very close to automatic writing, where again some unseen force guides the writer's hand. This activity has also been known to produce drawings as well.

Some who have become interested in this mystery board thought they were going to have fun with it. The fun later turned ugly when they found that a spiritual entity entered their lives. It became frightening for some too late when they realized they communicated with a force they were not able to control; a sure way for someone to become possessed.

It must be pointed out that mere interest and inquisitiveness to look into the unknown can be a person's undoing. The adventure into the unknown can be very frightening when participants discover they are unable to disengage from the experience. They become enmeshed with spiritually dark forces, which is not only extremely dangerous, but also forbidden by the Bible as well.

According to the Bible there are demonic powers at work in our dimension whose sole purpose is to confuse us, propagate lies, and to destroy us. The father of lies (Satan) is not a truth bearer! Demons simply use society's gullibility, ignorance and curiosity to lure people into a power trip. One of the major doctrines the Bible denounces, is demonology. Paul refers to this in Ephesians 6:12. Many scriptures refer to unseen evil intelligent forces at work. The Ouija Board is only another method of communication with those forces.

EXAMPLE ONE FROM THE RELIGIOUS CULT LIST

GAY CHURCHES

One of the subcultures of our society today is the homosexual movement. In just a short time, the phenomena of gay churches have shown up in several cities like Los Angeles, San Francisco, and Seattle. This is not a new event. The Biblical story of Sodom and Gomorrah is well known—yet the lessons from it are not accepted, even now.

Today, we see that the promotion of this activity is expected to be publicly tolerated and accepted as mainstream. This is a complex spiritual issue and not easily understood.

Gays look upon homosexuality as something they have been born with and not a lifestyle choice. Research on the origins of homosexuality swings far and wide and is essentially unsubstantiated. But Christians need only know what God has said on the subject. (1 Corinthians 6:9 states "Or do you not know that the unrighteous shall not inherit the kingdom of God? Do not be deceived; neither fornicators, nor idolaters, nor adulterers, nor effeminate, nor homosexuals...")

Labeling them as perverse has led many gays to display their hatred and venom for those who will not consider them "mainstream." Organizations like *Act Up*, *Dikes on Bikes*, and *Queer Nation* have far too much media

attention. Their parades in the cities are shameful acts,
taunting the public and flaunting their political agendas. They have entered into the legitimate church scene
as well as having established their own churches. Most
of the evangelical, fundamental and mainline Christian
churches do not condone what they stand for. Sadly
however, some do.

In 1989 the Catholic Church suffered a brutal attack at St. Patrick's in New York City. Militant homosexuals shouted and gestured obscenities at Cardinal
O'Connor as he was conducting Mass.[1] This attack was
part of their plan to undermine, disrupt, and destroy
the moral fabric of this society as represented by the
church and as established in God's Word. I believe the
gay movement is just another execution of the overall
Satanic plan to funnel people into the Luciferic Initiation through rebellion.

After many years as a charismatic prayer group leader,
I have seen very few converts from those in the gay
lifestyle. God died for them as well as for all sinners
and they can be saved. They do need our prayers, and
love. Our Love however, is not meant to show acceptance for unrepentant sin. Although the Catholic
Church was attacked for their stand against homosexuality, there are also some Catholic leaders with misplaced
compassion for gays. These leaders seem to accommodate and tolerate the sin as well.

A tactic often used by the gay society, for those who
disagree with them, is to label them as "hatemongers"
or "homophobics." Sincere Christians do not hate the
person, but the sin. Perhaps the depth of this issue can
be found in people who cannot separate the sin from
the person.

Persons who buy into homosexual deviancy also buy into the lie that says this conduct is "normal." It is a reversal of what God says in His Word.

EXAMPLE TWO FROM THE RELIGIOUS CULT LIST

NATIVE AMERICAN RELIGION

The Native Americans have quite a heritage. However, they are bound by many religious rituals and spiritual ceremony. Over the years, the American Indian tradition, has evolved to accommodate a white man's culture, which was forced on them. However, the invading white man's culture did little to change a belief system involving their heritage, folklore, and spiritual tradition. This race of people, who are proud, strong, and defiant, are bound to past traditions and to their ancestors. They practice a *shamanistic spiritism that keeps them from being free and able to deal with change. When some become Christian converts, they seem to be rendered ineffective because of continued ties to native American tradition and ritual.

Indians have been forerunners of channeling into the nether world through dance, hallucinatory drugs, and rhythmic chants. They did it before the New Age gurus ever entered the scene. Their belief that the earth is a living entity is being played out again by New Ager adherents with a fetish for *environmentalism. Excessive concern for the environment is becoming a religion itself. It seems we are only now catching up to Indian culture. In reality our culture is simply going backwards spiritually. It is another lie being propagated upon unwary people in today's "anything is acceptable world."

EXAMPLE ONE FROM TELEVISION AND MOVIES THAT PORTRAY:

PSYCHIC, SUPERNATURAL, AND SCIENCE FICTION THEMES

Many modern television and movie themes revolve around the occult. By the late 1930's, movies were introducing such characters as Dracula and Frankenstein. Mild in effect by today's standards, these movies frightened many an audience in their time. 1960 brought one of the all time thrillers to the screen in Alfred Hitchcock's, *Psycho*. Pictures like *The Exorcist* came in the early 1970's, followed by such terrors as *Poltergeist*, *The Amityville Horror*, and who could forget Freddie Kreuger in *Nightmare on Elm Street*, a gruesome piece of cinema replete with sequels.

Films of this nature open the mind to a kind of fear fascination with the Unknown. This is a demonic fear that does not go away easily once it attaches itself to a victim's mind. Television has catered to the appetite for the supernatural in its own part, recently introducing several programs like, *X Files*, for example, that deal with the phenomena of ghosts, aliens, and parapsychology in general. Sorcery is just another way Satan corrupts the minds of unsuspecting people. What better place to display the intrigue of this practice than in movies and on television!

All occultic activity is an abomination to God. Those who practice this sorcery will not enter heaven. The

Bible is very clear on this, and yet many people who have given themselves over to this form of witchcraft often quote Bible verses they claim support their activity. This approach does not stand the test of God's Word and will hardly be approved by Him. He will not be kind to sorcerers now or on Judgment Day.

EXAMPLE TWO FROM TELEVISION AND MOVIES THAT PORTRAY:

GRAPHIC VIOLENCE

Movies have taken great pains to build the "Super Hero" and in the process have established some pretty violent characters. Sylvester Stallone personified Rambo in the 1982 movie entitled, *First Blood.* Rambo was not alone in his portrayal of mindless mayhem. In 1984, Arnold Schwarzenegger laid the ground work for the part human, part robot figure in *The Terminator. Robocop*, another human/robot crossbreed, came out in 1987 and was so explicit in its violent scenes that throughout the country, fights actually took place outside the theater after showings of the film.

Physical violence is portrayed as overcoming evil in these type movies. Vigilantism was brought to its apex in a series of movies that followed the original, *Death Wish*. Here a citizen takes it upon himself to "clean up" society, Sending the message, "Who needs a God when a gun will do as well?"

The children raised in today's society are the rotten fruit of this mentality too. They are beginning to believe that packing a gun and killing people is normal behavior. This is evidenced in the countless episodes of shootings and stabbings taking place in schools and on the streets today in the 1990s.

Twenty-five years ago, movies had plots and good dialogue suitable for all the family to watch and hear. Today, dialogue is a steady stream of vulgar profanity steeped in a generous portion of illicit sexual situations. Television has sadly gone the way of movies, except for the "editing" out of what is now called, "strong language." Even kiddie cartoons have taken on an air of violence that researchers find have a "numbing" effect on small children.

Graphic violence is appealing to our fleshly nature and that's why it is hard to let go. This is another trap set by Satan, who is preparing us for The Initiation. This again is in direct opposition to the way scripture tells us to behave.

EXAMPLE THREE FROM TELEVISION AND MOVIES THAT PORTRAY:

SUBLIMINAL ADVERTISING

Subliminal messages are used to help create and develop markets for various products. The messages can be through sight or sound. It has been known for some time that a person can be influenced to buy a particular product or item, through the power of suggestion. Although the method is a proven one, it is not in the best interests of man to be so manipulated.

A well known western university presented a television program on the subject of subliminal messages. During the course of their investigation, they uncovered what appeared as faces that were subliminally used in one TV advertising scheme. The researchers did not know what the faces were supposed to do for product sales. However another person witnessing the program felt the faces looked like icons of the devil, or of demons.

It is possible that the icons were not meant to sell the product, but to subliminally suggest the desirability of the product is linked to demon characters associated with it. In other words—commercials can be used to sell the devil himself.

A few years ago, a similar activity discovered that some record albums were being recorded with back-masked subliminal messages. Some of the audible messages were clear enough to understand Satanic content.

Subliminal messages are effective, clever and have experienced a degree of success. The amount of subliminal activity that has been used on society is not known. I venture to say that it is Big Business for those who exploit it. I believe a similar mechanism is used by Satan and his willing human work force to influence mankind concerning spiritual matters. The Luciferic Initiation comes a step closer to mankind through yet another plot. Are we really sheep being led to the slaughter?

EXAMPLE FROM NEWSPAPERS, BOOKS, AND MAGAZINES THAT FEATURE:

PRO ABORTION MEDIA ARTICLES

Is there really such a thing as a victimless crime? This is what we are being told by the liberal media. All of society suffers from amoral activity, regardless of whether it's cooperative or private sin. Wrong is wrong and sin is sin, no matter how it's dressed up! The liberal media have for years taken the position that whatever people do in the privacy of their lives, homes, or bedrooms, are no one else's business. According to the teachings of the Bible, all of society suffers from sin and this includes sin that *humanism labels as victimless.

An example of what some say is a private matter is abortion. It's certainly not victimless for the woman or the child. Yet society is ready to say it's none of our business.

In the scientific community, there is a law that states "for every action, there is an equal and opposite reaction." If science recognizes there is a response due for a specific action, then we must realize there are social consequences for social actions. When we say, "It is my business, not yours," that is simply not true. This statement assumes there is no retribution against society for doing wrong. It fails to recognize that society is made up of the collective action of every person and their attitude (good or bad). Abortion effects everybody!

The media's constant dilution of moral values and the acceptance of liberal *situational ethics as "the norm," can not be accepted by any Christian. The media has proven themselves to be amoral. Is society to follow their example on how to live the good life? Just what is a the standard the public can use to see if the media is being honest or fair?

Abortion is nothing more than an outgrowth of a sin attitude. It is easier to bury beneath a person's conscience if the victim (helpless baby) has no voice. Thank God!—He knew what He was doing in the design of our bodies. However, some play God and hold the "*right*" to kill or not to kill. Does anyone really think they can dictate life choices without consequences? These ideas are prompted by Satan through the liberal media.

More and more people have accepted the act of abortion as a viable option. The only viable option is adoption, yet there is no media push on this simple solution. The enemy has already made deep inroads into the human race with demonic intelligence dressed up as compassionate simple answers to a very serious moral procreation problem. This kind of thinking moves a person in the direction of selfish rights; a step toward the Luciferic Initiation.

Man is continually being directed away from God. In the case of abortion, Satan has hidden sin behind convenience and a *right* called *Choice.* Choice is just a *"damage control word"* in an attempt to make killing babies look compassionate and clean. It is NOT so. Killing babies goes directly against God! Jesus can forgive the mother. God still loves the woman. He just hates the sin, as in the case of the homosexuals. As Christians we must not judge and condemn the Pro Choice activists. Instead, we should mirror the love of God as the proper alternative to the attitude that abortion is a good option. We must allow God to be the only judge in His sovereignty.

EXAMPLE ONE FROM CHURCHES THAT TEACH FALSE DOCTRINES:

EVERYONE GOES TO HEAVEN

The thought that people can go to hell is frightening. In light of this a new religious doctrine has been invented that allows everyone to get to heaven. If current religions do not permit everyone into heaven, then a New Age alternative "religion" has to be invented. The new idea is much more acceptable, than spending eternity condemned to an everlasting fire where everyone (in hell) is in torment. The Christian God is often portrayed as too mean, unforgiving or too hard to deal with.

New Agers are quick to point out that God is a God of love, but fail to acknowledge that He is also a God of wrath and judgment. The argument for them is that their "god" loves everyone in spite of sin and will forgive everything. This is partly true except they drop the part about repentance and turning away from their sin.

The enemy has veiled the heart of man so that he constantly looks for some other way to heaven, besides through God's son, Jesus. Demonic wisdom always works on the fears and weaknesses of man, providing alternative solutions (like soft love) for man to grasp and embrace. Failure to humble oneself at the Cross of Jesus allows a person to hold on to pride—the very sin that got Satan kicked out of Heaven! Through belief in New Age doctrines, a person becomes the image of Satan instead of the image of Christ; just the opposite of which our lives were originally destined!

Is there another way to Heaven? If so, no one has found it yet, although there are a multitude of philosophies and cults that claim other ways to heaven. Not one of these religions had a Savior who died for them, and then came back to demonstrate His power over death.

There have been erroneous Christian ministers in several different denominations who have written New Age material confusing people about their Christian faith. Some even propose alternative paths to God. From a Christian perspective, anyone promoting an alternative path to God is not in line with the Bible or its teachings. They are in all probability nothing more than a liar. Jesus warned us that if anyone comes by another way, he is a thief and a robber.

Simple, but strong faith in God provides inner strength and a peaceful heart for those who believe. Complex issues become simple with God given discernment, and are understood through faith. Our faith is not based on worldly knowledge or a higher cosmic consciousness, but by believing on Him who was sent—Jesus Christ of Nazareth.

EXAMPLE TWO FROM CHURCHES THAT TEACH FALSE DOCTRINES:

SOFT LOVE

What is "soft love"? It is when people believe it is okay to sin or experience anything one desires because God loves us so much that He will forgive anything. While God can forgive anything, there is first a requirement—it is called confession and true repentance.

Yes, God loves us, and He created us for His good pleasure. However, He does not want us to experience everything we are offered. He grieves when we take any road that will lead us away from Him...and that is what sin does. That road carries with it the risk that we may never make it back. Even so, He does not force us to love or accept Him. He is willing to wait and work with us through the circumstances of our lives. He hopes we will give up our selfish ways and patiently waits for us to come to Him for forgiveness, healing, and grace.

In the book of Isaiah (53:6), God states that, "Each of us has turned to his own way." This obviously bothered God. Today the modern equivalent is, "do your own thing." This popular phrase was the hallmark of the sixties and seventies promoted by the—"in generation" of the time.

Where did these self-serving thoughts come from? If God saw it as a problem several thousand years ago, then the source of these thoughts must be from His arch enemy. Again, worldly wisdom has cleverly brought many in opposition to God's Word.

Slowly and steadily, Lucifer has been moving humans away from God through the infusion of demonic rebellion. New Agers seem to forget that God said he disciplines those whom He loves. Discipline (a form of love) is necessary for Christians to be effective in His service. Without discipline, believers become "flaky" and less able to do the work of God. Not being reliable means that we cannot share in the grace that comes with voluntary obedience to Him. God knows how to get things done, but He requires us to be His *willing, disciplined* workers.

The same can be said for Satan and his workers, with one great exception. Satan *demands* obedience from his followers and *controls* all of their actions. God is the only one with promises for everlasting life and unimaginable heavenly things yet to be made known to us. Soft love is deceptive. It is a lie since the concept denies that we will be held accountable for our actions.

EXAMPLE FROM HUMANISM/MAN'S SOLUTIONS WITHOUT GOD:

SCHOOLS WHOSE POLICY IT IS TO:

Intimidate People having Religious Views

Frequent news accounts have reported on schools that forbid Christians to read or carry their Bibles. School principals, fearing the wrath of a few parents and the *ALCU who over react against students displaying a Bible or who pray in public. There is no constitutional requirement to ban God from school. The awesome power of a single Bible is demonstrated when it makes school officials react in terror. It just shows how much the enemy hates the ability and power of just one Bible and just one practicing Christian. Are children to be denied their right to religion just because a misguided precedent was set by the US Supreme court, in error?

Both visible and unseen powers are obviously shaken by a few Christians and their Bibles. There is a lot at stake and several organizations such as the ACLU, (and some church groups) want a complete separation of God and schools at any cost. I wonder if they are aware that they are fighting against God? How will they stand before Him in His court, where there are no lawyers or appeal? It is very possible they will be granted separation from Him as a final decision.

EXAMPLE FROM ART FORMS THAT SUPPORT THE KINGDOM OF DARKNESS:

MUSIC WITH HARD ROCK

Hard rock concerts seem to promote and encourages rebellion in youth. Wild body gyrations of the performers with their long hair and naked, sweaty chests are nauseating at best and certainly not edifying in any artful way.

Some hard rock bands have embraced satanic symbols and music lyrics that suggest and promote sexual-
ity, drug abuse, violence, and total disregard for traditional ethical values. As a result, several of these *fun*
events, cause people to behave like crazed animals who
may rape, stab, and even kill others. I would liken this
fun to a full blown riot at Attica, without the music.

In Bob Dylan's Christian album, "*Slow Train Com-*
ing," the title of the lead song is, "You Gotta Serve Somebody." It becomes abundantly clear that even in rock
concerts, you have to serve somebody. I wonder whom
the performers and the audience are serving? It certainly is not the God of creation, so it must be Satan.
There is no other reasonable answer. Rock concerts are
demonic praise and worship services for Satan. The
Bible tells us that God is enthroned upon the praises of
His people (Psalm 22-3). The same is true for Satan
and his cohorts who are also empowered by the music,
lyrics and crowds that attend these concerts.

I heard about one concert where a performer put
on a goat's head and let out a blood curling scream. Fear
seemed to flood the room and overwhelm the audience.
Many in the arena ran pushing and shoving their way
out through the exits. This act demonstrated how fear
was used as a set up to control the audience for a specific response. The event could have had a disastrous
outcome.

Many parents feel they have been betrayed. They
assumed rock concerts were harmless fun, and trusted
in a system that would magically look after their kids.
Not so! After reading about the unfolding events in this
book, I hope the reader begins to see that a multifaceted plan is starting to emerge which is meant to de-

stroy society. Not a good realization, is it? Could this be true or this just more radical Christian thinking? Please read on. Don't stop now—it's just beginning to get interesting.

DISCUSSION ON FIGURE 4-1—DEMONIC PATHS

Figure 4-1 is split into two halves. The upper half shows traditional demonic activities, known and labeled by the Christian church. The lower half is my attempt to describe demonic/alien activities that come through the New Age, not previously known or understood by the church or society in general.

It all begins with various inputs to the individual, as shown in the upper left circle. These inputs are things that we have to deal with in our everyday lives. The ones shown are labeled as evil in nature, although all inputs (good or bad) are subjected to the individual. All possible inputs on the Figure are not shown.

As you pass from left to right on the top half, you can see how a person can go from obsession, and then on through possession, eventually leading to destruction. Opportunities for release or deliverance can be obtained along the way. I will not spend much time on this upper half as it is somewhat understood by the average Christian. The lower half, however, is a different story.

For the New Age, traditional demonic activity has taken on a revised, sophisticated approach to influence and control, rather than move the person onto swift destruction. Instead, its approach is to capture and influence man for alien purposes. This is best done by getting mankind to use his intelligence and quest for knowledge to look into the unknown, accepting the explanations of the New Age teachings.

In the lower half, mere interest or inquisitiveness into the New Age approach opens a person's mind up to embrace a highly technical and delusional approach to man's problems. If followed as shown, the person can become a spokesman for demonic wisdom, rationally becoming a believer of things that are in opposition to God's teachings.

Although repentance is available for people who have under gone the Luciferic Initiation, repentance is very difficult since they do not recognize the deception. The New Age movement introduces the alien from outer space as a *Helper* or *Guardian* to us earthlings, though not all New Agers are aware of this yet. From published alien encounters, alien wisdom is highly intelligent and enticing as well as appearing beneficial. Later on in this book, I will cover the alien and flying saucer subject. Most documented alien incidents (or encounters) are devoid of a Christian God culture.

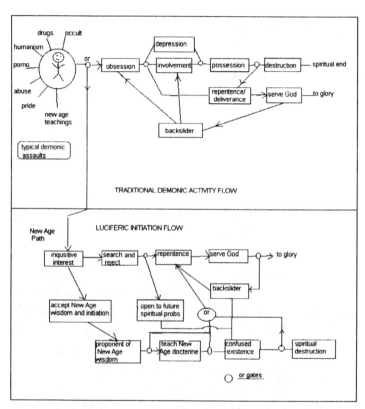

Figure 4-1
Demonic Paths

5

How Prevalent is the Luciferic Initiation?

Satan's influence on society is apparent, as can be seen from the items and examples provided in the previous chapter. Those who come under the influence of Lucifer experience a common event.

The influence is multifaceted, complex and integrated in society under many good sounding fronts, such as religion, entertainment and self-help programs. Satan's proponents (people who have been through the Luciferic Initiation) have found their way into the foundation of society's basic infrastructure.

The infrastructure I refer to includes organizations that make up our basic society as it has developed over many years. Organizations like schools (primary and secondary), colleges and universities, foundations, corporations, all levels of government, churches, and the basic family unit have been invaded. Here's the point— these influences are pervasive and already well established in all of societies' social functions.

If our social order fails to understand how the infrastructure is being manipulated and how to counter its effects, society will slip into the New World Order. In turn, this New World Order will force man into a new social environment; one filled with new approaches to civil, religious and human rights; I believe as we move toward these new approaches, things like patriotism and Nationalism will be forced to give way to the common good, or "universal goodness."

God's teachings will be an interference to the universal goodness of the new hierarchy. Surely this could translate into a new hell on earth. Not necessarily a burning hell, although cities engaged in riots might seem that way, but a place where weird, hellish doctrines would become precursors to the real hell. Our society may become a place where individual life must conform to the will of the group. Individualists (non-conformists) and politically incorrect religions, such as Christianity, will be a threat and justifiably eliminated like any undesirable commodity. This would include those who cling to patriotism and religious ideals which might disrupt the New World Order.

New Agers, unaware they are under another power (influence), believe they are promoting a social goodness that will benefit all of society. Their ungodly ideas are thought to be a creation of their own human reasoning and intelligence; causing these people to be difficult to reach through rational discussion. Without a Biblical standard, they can't separate their own ideas, from those inspired from evil sources.

As hard as it might be for a person to accept responsibility for themselves, it is even harder to admit being a sucker to some other power. It's a pride thing.

Christians, as well as non believers, have fallen into
this prideful kind of thinking. For many Christians going to church on Sunday morning is thought to be a
sufficient shield of protection against evil forces. However, if Christians do not have a serious relationship with
Jesus, as well as a strong understanding of Biblical values and a prayer life, they are apt to be deceived just
like anyone else. Without discernment (ability to know
what is God's and what is not God's), many fall into a
deception, believing doctrines and teachings outside
the Word of God. Hence, through ignorance, occultic
practices thrive within the body of Christianity.

In every major denomination, and non denominational church, there is ample evidence that New Age
teachings have crept into the basic belief structure.
Teachings such as: 1) There is more than one way to
God and heaven, 2) God wants you to be rich, 3) Astrology and psychic abilities are acceptable practices, 4)
Situational ethics and value's clarification are mainstream, 5) Soft Love and tolerance of sin is a desirable
Christian ethic, 6) Emphasis on humanistic values and
Liberation Theology. 7) and that more governmental
money will solve man's problems.

The basic structure of society and Christianity is
floundering under assault from the issues mentioned
in the preceding paragraph. I wonder if our world isn't a
parallel to the society that existed in Noah's time, before the great flood? Jesus indicated that signs for the
end of this age would be the same as in Noah's time
(Mat 24:38). That should give us something to think
about.

Ungodly forces of this age have been busy doing the
very thing that God said is hateful to Him; reversing

values in society by rejecting good for evil, and accepting evil as good. The success of this attack is apparent in good intentioned people, including many pastors, who are no longer able to discern right from wrong as conveyed by God's Word. They either do not know the teachings of the Bible, or no longer accept them.

The appeal of humanism, (often mistaken for human compassion) has such strong appeal, that promoting Biblical values seems out of date. Humanism and caring people, with all their worldly concern cannot become a replacement for God. The Luciferic Initiation has in large part, attained success in turning many away from Biblical teachings by creating a world's view of what is right and *fair*.

One day, I began to consider the growth and *quickening* of these New Age ideas. Many Christians I spoke with thought the roots of the New Age theology were formulated by a demonic spiritual network. This demonic network influences willing recipients in society.

This of course smacks of conspiracy. And we all know how conspiracies, fascinating as they may be, are viewed with a great deal of cynicism. For example, just look at the controversy surrounding the deaths of President John F. Kennedy, his brother Robert, and Dr. Martin Luther King. It is my belief that modern New Age writers, like Whitley Strieber, reveal a connection to an intelligent life force outside our world. Perhaps this force and influence comes from a UFO/Alien hierarchy; a hierarchy that is sometimes referred to as *Helpers, Watchers or Guardians*. We could be dealing with an unholy network of higher conscious beings who have been meddling in the affairs of man for ages.

It appears from Strieber's UFO books, and from many other abduction writers, that alien influence is on the rise. The sheer number of alien visitations and abduction reports attest to this fact. The Luciferic Initiation, defined in Chapter One, occurs daily according to events and experiences described in Strieber's best sellers, "*Communion*," and "*Transformation*." If Strieber and other similar writers are correct, then many people of this world already have been prepared and/or initiated into a strange intelligence network.

Concerning Strieber's many personal encounters with aliens, he describes events that bear on changing him and others, through some kind of a physical modification. A change, I claim, is tantamount to going through the Luciferic Initiation process. The initiation process is terrifying, and at times physical—but always mental and spiritual. Strieber developed a morbid acceptance for these alien creatures, but was not always comfortable with them. The alien encounter usually requires involuntary acceptance by the victim, with the *intent of networking with them.*

Other evidence pointing to the presence of unexplained forces working in our collective lives is found in the geometric circles, commonly known as Crop Circles. These circles continue to appear in the wheat and corn fields of England, France and North America. England has a reputable investigative organization, (the Center for Crop Circles Studies (CCCS) founded in 1990), that examines and performs serious investigation on this phenomenon.[1]

In *The UFO Report*, published by Avon, there was a section that discussed mystery circles. Under a topic entitled, "*A Religious Perspective*," the author pointed out a possible relationship between the circles and the New Age movement. The relationship goes something like this; In 1987, a medium named Isabelle Kingston belonging to a religious group called, New Era, in England, channeled messages while with her students. The messages came from a higher intelligence called the *Watchers and the Guardians*. When asked about the meaning of the circles, she was told by the channel spirit, "...the circles were made to prove the presence of the *Watchers*, who are connected to guiding humans in building the power needed to create the New Jerusalem..."[2] The event goes on to suggest that the *Watchers* have been coming to earth for many years and are engaged in bringing about the New Age, while networking with Man.

Many Crop Circles have been investigated and measured. They are perfect in geometric design, the flattened wheat is virtually undamaged, and seem to convey a message that no one on earth can read. Most of them appear overnight. Attempts to explain the circles have been offered, but remain essentially unknown as to what they are in a scientific sense. The circles are examples of a puzzling ongoing mystery that no one can adequately explain. In Greg Braden's book, "*Awakening to Zero Point,*" he attempts to interpret some of the glyphs based on his knowledge of "Sacred Geometry,"...what ever that is. This mystery of Crop Circles doesn't disappear like UFOs. They remain and are visible to the naked eye. In spite of the visible pictorial evidence, no one in the government seems interested.

The geometric designs have been examined by experts, and pictures are published in many periodicals. I'm not surprised to find that crop circles have an occult connection with the New Age movement. I can find no reference to such things in the Bible, or any connection to Jesus Christ and His second coming. The absence of any Bible connections should provide a solid suspicion about this strange phenomena for all Christians. The notion that there is an alien race standing by to "help" us here on earth, should make everyone a little nervous—if not highly skeptical.

Christians however, need not fear, God made a way for his people through the Blood of Jesus. Nevertheless, too many Christians are unaware that they are in potential danger because of their lack of knowledge. They have left themselves vulnerable to the manipulation of higher intelligent (demon) beings.

(Please note that I will refer, at times, to aliens and demons interchangeably. This is intentional and will become increasingly clear for the reader as we go along.)

As far as the New Jerusalem is concerned, any mention of a New Jerusalem without Jesus is an obvious hoax. The Bible is clear on this issue (especially as found in the book of Revelations). A logical question is: When did Jesus begin to give a "new" (additional) revelation, to support or counter the ones He has already given us? God is not a liar. He never contradicts His own Word! This "new" revelation concerning the new Jerusalem, comes from the *Guardians or Watchers*, (as mentioned in the UFO report) whoever they are. Isn't it strange that voices, through channelers, offer a new understanding or revelation about God?

If there really is a *Star Trek* type of space probe out there with aliens onboard carrying a prime directive for earth, it is probably referred to by Paul as, "*False Wonders*," (2 Thessalonians2:9) that appear in the heavens during the end time. I do not hesitate to believe that demonic "Powers" are standing by with orders from Satan to provide beautiful visual wonders which dazzle and overwhelm mankind as part of his attempt to replace God.

Why do you suppose the aliens are so secretive? What are they hiding? Perhaps the purpose is to hide their real plan from man!

6

Who is Susceptible to this Deception?

One afternoon, a Christian friend came to me in an agitated state. He was concerned that his brother had undergone the Luciferic Initiation.

Surprised at his statement, I asked, "How do you know this?" He mentioned, his brother went through a strange New Age treatment program. He went on to explain how his brother, a Born Again Christian who was having marital problems, sought counseling help from a Dominican nun located at a well-known university.

The counseling process included introducing the troubled young man to a therapy known as, "Physical Sculpture Therapy." As conveyed to me, the treatment requires a person to be alone in a room where they can release pent up emotions like crying, yelling, screaming, moaning, and jumping for some period of time. The object was to empty oneself and let the mind go blank. As a result of this treatment, something spiritual happened to this young man. He became enlightened, received a feeling of wholeness with the universe and developed inner light and peace...certainly a good feeling! This is an example of who can fall under the Luciferic Initiation experience.

Although the feeling resulting from this event appeared desirable, it became highly questionable as to what really happened to him. The feeling was characterized as somewhat euphoric. An inner light, peace and contentment was definitely experienced along with a feeling of being one with the world and the universe. This experience is what New Age proponents want us to achieve.

The event spoken about by my friend concerning his brother, demonstrates how even in the church (in this case the Catholic church) has been invaded by New Age theologies. Is it possible that the church has become hopelessly contaminated by ideas propagated by demons of enlightenment?

Through the New Age, multitudes of self-help programs and seminars have been introduced that on the surface seem beneficial. However, the training and methods often used are nothing more than a ruse for the alien spirits (*Watchers* or *Guardians*) to impart their deceptive "wisdom" to us. These powers and their associated intelligence are mentioned in Ephesians 6:12 by the apostle Paul, who refers to them as "...spiritual forces of wickedness in heavenly places." Could this power be directly associated with aliens, who are the hierarchy in the heavens, who also have a superior intelligence and a spiritual technology which can manipulate mankind?

God gave us free will and control over our decisions. We can use that free will for our benefit, or we can give it over to other powers. It is that simple.

These other powers are not necessarily intelligent life forms from some distant galaxy in the universe. Over the years, science fiction writers have created imaginary worlds somewhere in outer space—places where higher life forms and superior intelligence exist. This might be acceptable if there was no God and we just happened to belong to some structured part of the evolving universe. Carrying this scenario further, other "universe citizens" (aliens) might come along to show us new ways and a new technology to live by. They could also use us for their own selfish purposes, or even destroy us. How are we to know? However, if there is a God and He established the rules for the heavens, including the earth and all the galaxies, then we should pay attention to what He says in His written Word. We could (must) avoid falling into the trap of our lives.

In Ephesians 6:12, the Apostle Paul said, "...For our wrestling is not against flesh and blood, but against principalities and the powers, against the rulers of the darkness of this age, against spiritual hosts of wickedness in the heavenly places..." Paul's all encompassing statement is not just talking about some intangible thing. He speaks of powerful entities existing in the heavens. I believe this is a reference to the so-called *Helpers, Watchers or Guardians*, often referred to by New Agers as guides.

These so-called guides are sometimes referred to as other "*christs*," or *Ascended Masters from higher astral plains of existence. There is a grim possibility that they are "helping" earth people evolve into spiritual clones of the demonic kingdom. (When man connects with these beings, who knows for sure what he is being evolved into, or the full extent of their spiritual experimentation?)

If aliens had an honorable purpose, they would have revealed themselves long ago so that man could question and investigate them from an ethical, moral, and Judeo/Christian perspective. I do not believe they will reveal themselves for who or what they really are, (a force leading people away from God) until they have thoroughly prepared us to receive them as heaven sent helpers. Exposure of their intent would remove their control over us, and I suspect alert mankind to resist them. At any rate, it would hinder their accessibility to us.

There is a current fascination over angels and many books on the subject are now available. The Bible clearly shows in many instances that God has angels who work for Him and are sent to aid His people here on earth (Heb. 1:14). God's angels will not play games with your mind and body, or give you a secret ride on a flying saucer. They will not fill you with terror and strange experiences that have no connection with the Creator. God's angels certainly would not violate a person's body by performing surgery, altering brains, sticking long needles into the abdomen, and performing offensive sexual invasions. There are many books, stories and personal accounts that report these types of encounters. I believe the "alien helpers" are nothing more than the "fallen angels" referred to in the Bible. Throughout the Bible, there is no evidence of God's angels performing these morbid types of behavior.

Nothing on this physical earth is without some tinge from the unseen world; perhaps more real than the hot dog we eat, or the car we drive. Things we possess in this world are very temporal and even heaven and earth will one day pass away; but what is carried within the heart will endure for all eternity. So, perhaps we should consider the real challenge, the unseen world that surrounds us.

New Age Thinking

New Age thinking can be traced back a long way. For example, Plotinus, the philosopher, lived between 203 and 270 A.D. He possessed knowledge of the spirits and could predict the future. His ideas are still being embraced today, in dealing with the world as a *being*. Today we hear a great deal about the *living earth*. But I wonder where the heart is? In Genesis, God instructs man to use and take care of the earth, but does not instruct us to *worship* the earth.

The idea that a single man or group of men over the ages developed the true philosophy of life leaves a treasure chest filled with error and half-truths. Outside a proven standard like the Bible, there is no correct path. Many today are adrift with no real purpose, chasing after some vague concept or another concerning the meaning of life. Christians also will soon be faced with some very hard choices concerning their faith and the future.

It is not hard to show how Satan can use a mixture of philosophies, alternative values, false prophets, visionaries and futurists to create confusion. He is the master proponent of conflict and confusion. It should not be a surprise to see many groups disagreeing with each other—even in the New Age movement.

A person who does not use the Bible as a measure for values is very susceptible to being a victim of the New Age mentality. This does not leave the Christian without a problem either. Christians who are uninformed, naive, and dabble in the occult or New Age teachings do so at their own peril! It is imperative that we not only know the Bible, but understand it and embrace it as our standard. We must focus our hope on Jesus, the author and finisher of our faith. To do any less may prove eternally *fatal.*

The Bible, as a standard takes on new meaning for even those who are skeptical of its inspired authenticity. A newspaper article covered research findings from mathematicians who found hidden word patterns in the Biblical account of Genesis. It suggests that the Old Testament Books, are the work of a divine author. By treating Genesis as a long cryptographic string of letters with no spaces between words, they searched for hidden word patterns in the text. What they found were words like "Zedekiah," (a king of Judah during the sixth century B.C.), and "Matanya," Zedekiah's original name.

The article indicated that the capacity to weave so many meaningfully related, randomly selected word pairs in a text with a coherent surface meaning is beyond the capacity of any human being. These findings have been published in the secular society's "Journal of the Royal Statistical Society," and in the Journal "Statistical Science."[1] Their findings all point to a divine author.

Are Christians Susceptible?

An example of how the New Age ideologies have crept into the church scene was demonstrated by a minister who called in on a New Age radio talk show. While listening to the program one night, I came to realize the meaning of how the Elect can be led astray.

The radio host interviewed a person about the meaning of chaos theory and spiritual planetary experiences. One caller said he had been a minister of the gospel for many years and experienced many spiritual things. He then explained that his experience was through the Holy Ghost. At that point, I thought he was pretty much on target.

He then went on to say that at times, he would feel the power of God come down over him and take control of his hand. He would ask questions and if the answer was yes, his hand would move in a small circle. If the answer was no, then his hand would move back and forth in a straight line. This is a classic case, of how a person can believe in the Gospel of Jesus and still be deceived by ungodly spiritual forces, through the crude use of *occultic automatic writing.

On another talk radio program, a person called in and claimed to be a Christian—and a psychic! These are incompatible terms. Another example of how Christianity is being mixed with the occult was described by a woman who practiced mingling white witchcraft with the Bible and the cross of Jesus Christ. Her perspective was:

"We believe everything comes from a higher source—I call it God," ... *"We can still believe in God and Jesus and still practice some form of witchcraft. We bless the Bible, and all of us wear crosses. We don't do anything offensive."*[2]

The apostle Paul asks, "How can light and darkness live together?" These are blatant cases of people thinking they are serving God while justifying and embracing ungodly occultic practices. Thirty years ago, no one imagined the idea of mixing Christianity and the occult. The fear of the heavy hand of God was prevalent. Obviously today, things have changed.

The Bible does not provide compromising or conflicting direction on the occult—it is resolutely condemned. People who mix Christianity and the occult run the risk of the loss of their souls. Worse however, is that they spread the "disease of the soul" to others who might join them. We either build the Kingdom of God or the Kingdom of Darkness. There is no other place or neutral ground to take a stand.

Susceptibility

Children are not exempt from the quagmire of the Luciferic Initiation...especially those in public schools. At the end of the school year, I know of a mother who was going through her child's school bag only to find several sheets of "Relaxation exercises" that were definitely of New Age origin. These exercises were introduced and used by the school psychologist to get the students to relax. However, review of the material showed it to be an introduction to eastern yoga and mind meditation type exercises.

The mother was alarmed about the mention of the "helper within" that was referred to, as an *ally*, whom the child could communicate with. This "helper" was someone old, wise and someone he could trust. An *imaginary being* they could feel safe to be around. There were several exercises and each one led deeper into a relationship with this *imaginary being*.

This approach is similar to the method used to receive a spirit guide and to learn channeling—all of which are New Age teachings. This mother's concern, was brought to the principal of the school, and the principal claimed no knowledge of the New Age material being used. This incident highlights how easy it is for New Agers to affect children in public schools.

Susceptibility seems to be tied to a person's recep-
tiveness to occulti. People struggling under the
Luciferic Initiation often do so without the knowledge
that they have done anything wrong. For some, however, the struggle seems to carry with it terms like,
"higher consciousness," planetary consciousness (the
environmental emphasis), other lives, *karma, psychic
abilities, harmony with the one, and so forth.

The difficulty in working with people under the
Luciferic Initiation, comes from their lack of knowing
that they have become a victim at all. An example that
comes to mind are a few people who are very unstable.
They may have been in and out of institutions—and
claim to be Christians. They float from job to job, and
church to church. All the while their mental health continues to worsen. When these people talk about God,
it is a god who gives them physical powers or transcendental experiences. When asked about other important Christian factors like humility and *agape love, they
would indicate they are important; however, these factors are not evident in their life.

Discerning the Truth

In attempting to locate an indication of a person's
susceptibility, it will require a good ear, and Godly discernment, to make an accurate determination. This
can be demonstrated in a person's expected response
to his prayer. Occasionally one hears how God answered
prayer in a miraculous way. However, everything spiritual has to be examined carefully and possibly considered as coming from another god before being accepted.
For some, it may be hard to correctly assess the truth

because the enemy has so disguised his influence that it is hard to discern the truth.

For years, I did not understand why certain individuals could not improve their Christian growth on a consistent basis. Problems with excessive energy, anxiety, instability and personal failures seem to plague many of them. After assessing these factors, it became apparent to me that many probably underwent the Luciferic Initiation experience at some time in their lives. The most disturbing part of the dilemma was the inability of a troubled person to separate God from any god; the Biblical God from the masquerading god. While thinking they are serving God, spiritual evidence would suggest they are serving Satan unaware. The initiation can be so veiled and so good that it's impossible for a secular counselor and difficult for most Christians to detect.

The Initiation Mechanism

New Ager, Greg Braden, author of "*Awakening to Zero Point,*" discusses a type of initiation as a factor of earth's magnetic field strength.[3] It goes something like this: When someone enters into a lesser magnetic field strength than the earth's, (like in upper rooms of the pyramid of Giza), they have the opportunity to harmonically change the frequency of every cell in their body. This event is somehow directed by a person's will. As the person chooses to think differently of themselves under these lesser magnetic fields, they can consciously alter every cell in their body, affecting their mind and spirit. The person desiring this experience by vibrating to a higher level of consciousness, does not have to go to Egypt for it. The experience can be had anywhere the person desires.

The problem with the mechanics of this thought transforming event, is that it does not consult the will of God. It is an experience of merging with the, "ultimate one" (whoever that is), and I'm sure it is not God. A Christian who prays, experiences a similar effect. But God's grace sets the standard. God did not define the mechanism for us, He simply told us how to do it.

The ungodly initiation mechanism depends on a person's will, and their desire to receive the knowledge offered them through extra sensory consciousness. In my opinion, this is just another way to experience the *Luciferic Initiation.*

In my attempt to demonstrate this simple mechanism I have developed several graphics that show how mystical energy flows from both God and Satan. Note in Fig. 6-1 that the flows are similar but are *phase shifted from each other. The alignment also affects a person's spirituality. This simple graphic demonstrates how a person can be influenced by one flow or the other, and which force they are in tune with. Figure 6-2 describes a person who is caught up in worldly affairs, but is really under Lucifer's influence. The enabling energy is directed by a person's choice as noted in the graphic. Notice how this person can telegraph his thoughts by his desire. Through prayer godly people (in figure 6-3) also telegraph their desire (obedience) and find favor by receiving God's grace energy.

Vibrational energies, resonance, and higher consciousness often stressed by the New Agers are simply occultic effects resulting from Luciferic phased energy flows. It is an ability for the unwary to plug into ungodly spiritual intelligence. Figures 6-4 and 6-5 show a close up of cell alignment phased to the energy flow. It also reveals who the person holds allegiance to. Figure 6-6 shows why many Christians suffer difficulties in their life. It's primarily because an area of their lives are still under Lucifer's influence (shown by the opposite phase shift). This figure also explains why so many Christians never experience victory over certain personal problems. There are many variations of this figure. Can you determine some of them?

Who is susceptible to the Luciferic Initiation? The answer is really quite simple. Anyone who does not have a *close* personal relationship with Jesus is fair game for these ungodly, mind bending powers.

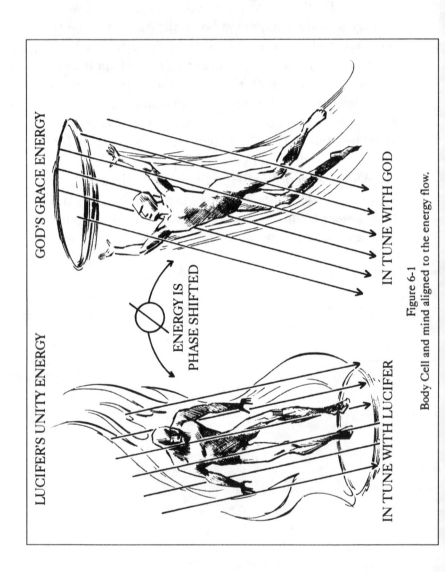

Figure 6-1
Body Cell and mind aligned to the energy flow.

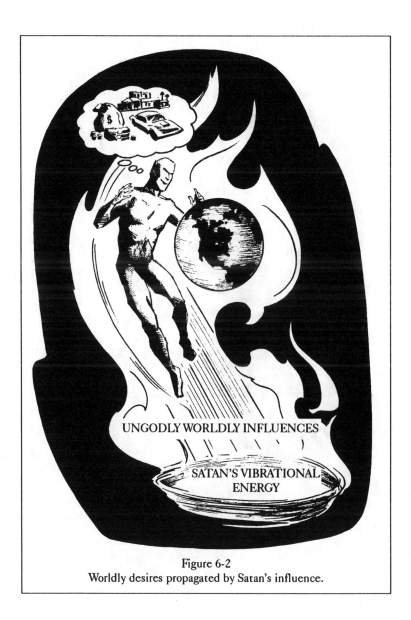

Figure 6-2
Worldly desires propagated by Satan's influence.

Figure 6-3
God sends grace (help) through prayer.

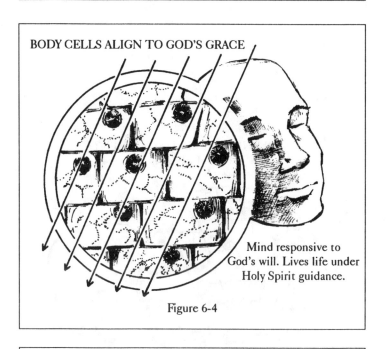

BODY CELLS ALIGN TO GOD'S GRACE

Mind responsive to God's will. Lives life under Holy Spirit guidance.

Figure 6-4

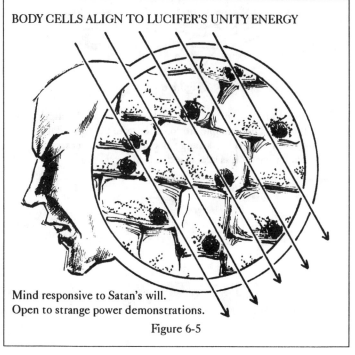

BODY CELLS ALIGN TO LUCIFER'S UNITY ENERGY

Mind responsive to Satan's will.
Open to strange power demonstrations.

Figure 6-5

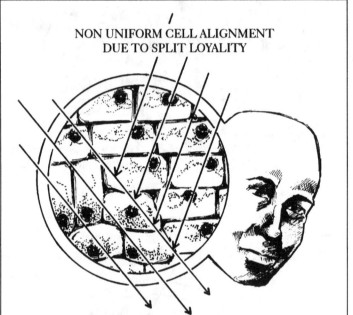

NON UNIFORM CELL ALIGNMENT
DUE TO SPLIT LOYALITY

Figure 6-6

Note: This person has part of their life under Lucifer's influence. These people are confused as to the truth. They are open to receive strange occultic experiences even though they profess allegiance to God.

7

The Strange World of UFOs

Alien occurrences reported by Whitley Strieber in the books "*Communion*" and "*Transformation*" were partly responsible for prompting my desire to look into these events from a Christian perspective. After reading these popular best sellers, it became clear to me that someone or some unknown force, perhaps extraterrestrial, was meddling in world affairs. These books are clever, creating the illusion that some beneficial force will take us by the hand, and lead us into the shady abyss of a new way of life.

Whether through space aliens, demons, or unknown powers from on high, strange doctrines seem to be creeping into society that take us away from Biblical perspectives. How exciting it must be for those who participate in this high adventure of a mysterious unknown. I would think somewhere along the way they would come to their senses and see the perilous road ahead. After all, not all alien adventures end like a Star Trek episode. For those unable to see the dangers, the alien experience will introduce man to spiritual influences that lure them into thinking they can be participants in their own destiny. Sadly, this kind of thinking can only leave a person open to heresy and disappointment.

In the movie, "*Out on a Limb*," Shirley McLain stood on the seashore with a friend shouting, "I am God!" I wondered at the time why she didn't try walking on the water. It might have awakened them both to the fact that they were, "just all wet." This issue brought to mind David Spangler, a prominent new age writer, who espouses that very notion ...To say, "I am God," is to simply affirm that I am one part, like everything else."[1] That idea is a form of pantheism, meaning that God is part of everything created. Perhaps this is where the idea of unity and oneness comes from.

While reviewing "*Communion*" and "*Transformation*," I became keenly aware of why people are innocently used as tools of an unknown intelligent force—(a spiritual enemy perhaps). In addition, these books dramatize how a person can be "luciferized" and fail to recognize what is happening. Clues about Luciferic mysteries are usually evident but, as clear as the clues might be, they are not always detected by the participant. An example of this was expressed by a woman at a conference Strieber attended. She suggested his alien encounters could be initiatory in nature; "a journey into the darkness where the secrets of the spirit are kept."[2] Her comment should have alerted Strieber that something might be wrong.

The impact of Strieber's extraterrestrial books (and similar accounts from other authors) on society, and their overwhelming popularity, cannot be taken lightly. If the published accounts are true, then mainstream Christianity, out of necessity, is required to seriously step up to the issue and review the incidents from the perspective of God's Word.

The Bible does not clearly or specifically address flying saucers or aliens per Se. What is the average God fearing person to do? It's not time for despair, however. This issue is not hard to sort out; for it *is* covered in the Bible. We need to remember the words of the Apostle Paul in 2nd Thessalonians 2:9, when he said, the end time would include, "signs and false wonders." Recent strange events seen in the heavens could be what he was referring to. If so, popular embrace of UFOs and aliens have the potential to mislead many. Or as the Bible suggests, mislead even the elect—if it were possible!

Several major newspapers in the United States, such as the *Dow Jones News, Houston Chronicle, Boston Herald, New York Tribune, Detroit News,* and many others, ran somewhat positive reviews about the book, "*Communion.*" Comments ran the gamut from, "a convincing case," to "his book deserves to be taken seriously."[3]

Why Strieber was selected for these alien visitations is not clear to me, but several reasons surface in my mind and are discussed in this chapter. Strieber went to great lengths to prove that he was not just a kook writing another sci-fi novel. He carefully selected a psychiatrist to help him; one not previously involved with alien phenomena. By submitting to hypnosis sessions, he was able to bring out details that occurred during the visitations. This process enabled him to authenticate his sanity and sort out what was happening to him.[4]

During the hypnosis sessions, he was eventually made aware of others like himself who also met in group sessions to cope with similar alien visitations. Their encounters all had a ring of familiarity. In the following critique, I refer to a few of his experiences for the purpose of questioning the alien motive behind the event.

Critique of "Communion" and "Transformation":

In the book, "*Communion*," the writer recounts his experiences with alien visitations and abductions in great detail. He describes his abductors in specific color size and shape. Early in the book, aliens tell him he has been physically changed (modified), but they don't tell him the reason.[5]

He was taken aboard spacecraft often, and having frequent alien visits that took place in his upper New York State cabin. He described various types of aliens. Some were tall and thin, some short and wearing blue coveralls, some gray, some with large dark round eyes, and some with large tear shaped eyes. There were also aliens who appeared human like.

He described his initial encounter as somewhat fearful and scary. During repeat visits, he found that he was helpless and under their complete control. His abductors said, "You are the chosen one..."[6], though why he was chosen they never made known to him. During an early encounter, he underwent a probing of his genitals and a physical examination. At one point when a probe was inserted through his nose to his brain, he is informed that his metabolism had been altered and he would not live long if he ate sweets. Even worse things, like death, would result if he ate chocolate.[7] These statements were not true statements, as he later found out.

Feeling that his sanity might be slipping away, he carefully selected a psychiatrist to help him understand what was happening. After several visits to the analyst, he began to piece together a remarkable story of alien visits. Surprisingly, through hypnosis he discovered some of the alien visits dated back several years. At one point, he seemed to question the intention of these aliens, even considering the possibility that they might be evil. However, the thought was so disturbing that he discarded the idea.[8] I find this a point of curiosity. Why is it so hard to face the truth, even when it may be unpleasant? What a pity he did not pursue this very real possibility.

I believe the author was selected and programmed with their data as he went through an intense Luciferic Initiation.

Once, however, while under their influence and control, an unusual fact emerged. He challenged them by asserting, *"they had no right,"*[9] *(to violate him*—emphasis mine). They countered, *"we do have a right " (to do what we are doing—emphasis mine)*. An obvious question is: Who gave them this right and by what authority are they able to violate him, or anyone for that matter? If it was not God (which obviously it was not), then their "authority must have been Lucifer himself.

It is my contention that this man was selected and brought under their influence for several reasons. The primary one being that he is intelligent and had a successful, professional writing background. Strieber has a writing style that is strange, and along the lines they were looking for. I believe the aliens networked with him, knowing he would creatively write about his strange experiences. The purpose would only be known to them. This plan could be as simple as desensitizing the human attitude toward aliens. Strieber may have been a "control case" (perhaps one of many) used to prepare earthlings to receive alien involvement in their lives. Commandeering the mind and professional experience of a best selling author could only help their cause. After all, perhaps it's part of the alien time table, to entice man into the mystery of these trans-dimensional ships and their cargo of aliens.

After many visits, he had one particular experience where he found himself in a room filled with aliens who looked as if they might be from a higher alien command. Several tall aliens, appearing translucent white congregated around another alien who appeared to be a high official. Strieber was prepared for this meeting, by being stripped of his clothes and made to wear a white paper-type gown. Oddly, when the meeting started, he was asked to explain the reason for the fall of the British Empire. As he stood before them, he shocked himself by explaining the collapse of the British empire in the greatest of detail. He exhibited an extraordinary and surprising knowledge of the subject. When he had finished, there was a long silence that eventually gave way to many favorable comments by the aliens.[10]

The question that comes to mind is: Why would the fall of the British Empire be of any consequence to aliens from space? After pondering this question for some time, I began to realize that this particular event was in all likelihood a *test* the aliens were conducting. A test, where they were checking the accuracy of the information that *they* had previously installed into Strieber during their "modification" procedure.

According to Strieber, a significant number of people in the world have already been "modified" and continue to be "evolved," as the aliens put it. I am convinced that Strieber's modification event is evidence of being spiritually and physically marked through the Luciferic

Initiation process. This process ensnares humans into the Luciferic web—it brings them into Satan's service.

Who Are These Earthlings?

The answer to this is elusive for anyone to completely understand or determine, but I think it may lie in two basic types of people: 1) those who don't know Jesus. This category is represented by agnostics, atheists, occultists, users of black and white magic, and people who believe they are "in control" of their own lives, not attached to any religious belief system. 2) The second type is made up of those who have a religious belief system, but are also open to the new age philosophies. The second type *can* include "Christians." Unhappily, this might represent a large segment of the churched population.

An assumption is often made that Christians have the wisdom and discernment, to avoid dabbling in the dark regions. After observing the Christian circles I travel in, I have found that this is not always the case. Wisdom and maturity that comes from knowing the Bible, and involvement in a solid gospel teaching church, helps prevent the loss of souls to baneful, intelligent powers. Protection from these powers is not assured, if believers allow New Age ideas to infiltrate their lives. Usually though, fellowship with Christians grounded in Christian principles, provides a safety net and buffers one from accepting New Age ideals. A Biblical proverb assures us; there is safety in many counselors.

In the book, "*Transformation,*" Strieber reveals additional information, about encounters mentioned in "*Communion,*" as well as other frightening extraterrestrial adventures. He expands on an earlier experience he had with high alien command officials concerning the discourse on the British Empire. He remembered being led to a particular place in the room where he was to speak and noticed that the aliens all had gauze over their eyes and chins. One could only speculate why the gauze was used, but perhaps we smell or look unpleasant to them. They certainly appear unpleasant to earthlings! According to Strieber, the leader was extremely formal and exuded an air of contempt—hardly a Godly quality.

As mentioned earlier, after Strieber spoke on the fall of the British Empire, there was a lull that was followed by many positive responses. However, he perceived a touch of *irony* in their comments. Afterwards, he was led down a neutral gray and tan corridor by two dark blue beings, which also wore dark blue coveralls. These particular aliens were described as being about three and one-half to four feet tall, having haunting and sinister faces.

Strieber had an eerie feeling concerning the drawer-lined corridor he was led through, as if it was conscious— or alive. While in the corridor, his escorts stopped and opened one of the many drawers that lined the corridor. To his shock and amazement, he saw a stack of alien bodies, all exactly alike. Each body was encased in a kind of cellophane covering! This "favor" shown him by his escorts, clued him to the possibility, that aliens may exist in some other form.[11] Perhaps they put on body masks to enter our dimension. These packaged bodies could represent an interesting revelation; one that suggests a technical and spiritual ability to change their appearance as they move in and out of various dimensional environments.

If the idea of packaged alien bodies is not far-fetched enough, in both *"Communion"* and in *"Transformation,"* the aliens claim they can move souls from one body to another![12] Can they do that? Is this possible? If so, perhaps that's the reason for the stack of alien bodies. I do not believe they have this ability with human souls. This also substantiates their demonic origin, explaining why at some crash sites we have found alien bodies, but not demons themselves. (Demons are spirit and not physical.)

At one point, Strieber thought something was moving behind the large eyes of these creatures. Is the real life substance of the alien inside the visible body? Perhaps they can only exist in our dimension through the use of masks designed to drape over a spirit body, or they desire to further mislead us by making us think they need bodies to survive. Another theory might be, a need to cover themselves with a protective suit to screen out earthly contamination. Who knows for sure?

Another peculiar response the author spoke of during his encounters with the aliens, was a tingling sensation that ran through his entire body, preceding the arrival of the alien. As marvelous as the sensation was, he always had a sense of relief when it was over.[13] Could this sensation be the result of a transducer implant used to enhance telepathic communication, providing control over a human subject they were about to visit?

Strieber recounted that at one point, he felt he was entering a struggle greater than life and death. In fact, he thought it might be a struggle for his soul, or at least that eternal part of him. He comes to a consensus that there may be worse dooms than death.[14] Jesus tells us not to fear those who can destroy the body, but rather God, who can destroy both the body and soul. It is not

ironic that a person so involved with alien forces as
Strieber is, to come up with a "doom" realization. (Perhaps these demons were vying for his unsaved soul.)

Now, if we could get Christians to realize there is a
doom worse than death perhaps we could re-focus our
Christian energy on God's principles instead of our own.

Evidently, the idea that these encounters might be
inspired by demons or demonic intelligence, was not
accepted by the author, scientists, or the doctors working with him. They believed they were beyond such
things. Their education and training definitely clouded
their perceptions. While training and intellect can prepare us for the work we do here on earth, it is woefully
lacking in preparing us for discernment of spiritual
matters. The Bible is the only manual revealing the
truth about discerning spirits, and spiritual warfare.

Strieber indicates that after his two books were written, he again struggled with the notion that aliens might
be evil. Although again, he foolishly discarded the idea
and wrote his third book on the alien subject, *"Break-
through."*

Jesus said, *"And you shall know the truth and the truth
shall make you free."* (John 8:32) Why then, do some people
listen to strange ideas and thoughts that prevent them
from developing a spiritual sensitivity to hear the truth?
Men of science, who are always attempting to approach
strange and mysterious events from every possible avenue, should not overlook the various religious angles
as well. Perhaps they would learn that all truth does
not fit under a microscope or come out of a laboratory
experiment. How distressing it will be on that one day
when closed darkened minds, will find the real truth
too late.

One morning, Strieber and his wife were chatting at breakfast. He realized that when his wife would ask questions about the aliens—such as, "Why did they come here?"[15] and "Where are they from?"[16] a voice would speak to him in his right ear. After some time, he noticed that the voice was no longer at his right ear, but moved within him, as in switching to thought mode. He suspected that the feeling was similar to channeling.[17]

The answer to the question, "why are they here?" was astonishing! (The voice answered), "We saw a glow,"[18] was the reply. Could this glow be the glow that God puts into every soul and created person? Another explanation, might be the glow that came from the radiation cloud which resulted from atomic testing that started in Nevada in 1947.

One UFO researcher made an interesting point, noting a sharp increase in sightings since the 1947 atomic testing. Incidentally, modern ufology began with disk sightings around Mt. Rainier about the same time. The dramatic increase of documented sightings, and alien experiences since the late 1940's can hardly be ignored or dismissed, as the rambling on of unstable people.

Is it possible that sophisticated and technically superior beings have found a way to enter and corrupt God's creation? Why would they want to do that? Well, let us speculate that aliens are synonymous with fallen angels. If so, they might be disfranchised angels, who can no longer have fellowship with God. Humankind certainly can't be very popular with them, especially if God intends that we are to someday replace them.

I believe a credibility problem exists with the notion that aliens might be benevolent souls hovering about over our heads, giving us a "helping" hand. So far, they have given us nothing tangible, and certainly nothing that enhances our relationship with the Creator.

According to Strieber, the year 1968 brought about one of the most startling episodes that he ever endured. He actually disappeared from earth for several weeks. Living in London at the time, he had decided to travel to several different countries, on the European continent. Once in Rome, he found himself touring the Vatican Museum, a sight to behold, with many art treasures. At the museum he saw something that brought on an intense, overwhelming fear. He fled the city as fast as he could. Taking several trains, Strieber found himself in Barcelona, Spain. There, he secluded himself in a back room of a hotel and only went out at night.

According to him, his memory became totally fragmented at that point. He remembers, a woman giving him a ticket for a flight on Egypt-Air. Many flights were offered to students on that airline at the time. He recalls entering a flight vehicle through a door in the floor. While on board, he noticed the air had a nasty smell, like a sulfurous privy. Later, when he disembarked through the same door in the floor, he came face to face with aliens in a place that looked like a desert oasis. The oasis was bordered with tall, thin trees surrounded by a vast desert under bright tan skies.[19]

Several bizarre occurrences took place at this desert location, one of which, was his introduction to the *"university."* The aliens told Strieber the desert university was a million years old! Where in the galaxy were they? Certainly not on any earthly plain where humans normally live.

A specific adventure began for him when he was led into one of the university rooms overlooking the desert. After stepping into a circle on the floor, he was overcome with a very great urge to dance! According to his account, he danced and danced without stopping, while at times he found himself inside the lives of other people.[20] He claims to have passed through a multitude of lives. This event appears to be a kind of possession (a spirit taking possession of other lives), sharing memories or other life experiences these demons had recorded and stored from previous victims of abduction. It may have been a kind of "channeling" event Strieber underwent.

When this desert experience was finally over, he found himself back in London, wondering how he had managed to return. A most amazing fact unveiled itself when his friends informed him that he had been missing for several weeks!

Let's take a closer look at what might be going on in this series of events. The first clue I find is his panic stricken behavior after seeing something in the Vatican Museum. Believe it or not, that something was an old stuffed owl! What could be the meaning of a dead, stuffed owl? For starters, it seems the owl has some esoteric quality associated with occultic activities. The author mentioned "owl imagery" is persistently connected to alien visitor experiences. Owl imagery experiences have been verified by others sharing similar experiences. Why this occurrence was so traumatic is not exactly clear. Although it could have been a mental triggering mechanism, sometimes referred to as a screen memory. He also indicates that the word owl, in Latin is "strix," which is another name for witch. Evidence of an occultic connection just seems to get bigger.

Apparently, the aliens can change form and even take on the appearance of other living creatures, such as owls.

It might be a spiritual cloaking ability to prevent man from seeing them as they truly are. No doubt, Strieber unconsciously knew the owl represented a powerful threat from past extraterrestrial visits. That was the probable reason he reacted the way he did by departing Rome in a state of panic.

The second clue is his cryptic flight to some strange land. It began when a mysterious woman came to his room in Barcelona and gave him an airline ticket. Upon receiving the ticket, he later boarded an alien craft. His ride to the "desert" was hardly normal. He remembers another "person" on board who looked after him, administering a strange liquid to his tongue when he became nauseated. While on board, he noticed a smell of a sulfurous privy. Numerous references to hell are made by writers who often mention sulfurous smells. Could there be a connection?

After landing and disembarking the craft, he saw aliens and a strange bright tan sky, a desert with tall thin trees—definitely a place unlike this world. I believe, the vast desert scene is another clue. (Jesus did speak of demons being driven out of people into dry places in Matthew 12:43).

The author had many other penetrating experiences that seem to be out of our reality scope. There were strange sensations, foul smells, and insect-like creatures (demons) that seemed to mother him.

On one occasion, while visited by these horrible insect aliens, they transported him to a place where he was given the opportunity to witness the punishment of another alien. The alien appeared as a normal human, and received a severe beating with whips until he was completely slumped over. The sight of the beating left Strieber very shaken. A voice told him that the beating was administered because of the alien's failure to properly influence Strieber during a particular incident.[21]

Were they trying to lay a guilt trip on Strieber for control purposes, or were they demonstrating how "benevolent and kind" they were? The whole incident seems to be straight from the kingdom of hell; a place devoid of forgiveness and one of severe punishment. Individual decision making, or accommodation for failure does not seem to be part of the alien scene.

These ruthless creatures have shown in every possible way, their disregard for our well being. If they are indeed fallen angels or demons, they have been already judged by God, fighting with a disciplined purpose to bring in their "New Age" for Man. This anti-God struggle will become more intense as the end time approaches.

Through all of this, Christians have a great opportunity to overcome the struggle while here on earth. We have the honor to become co-laborers with Jesus and help defeat the mayhem planned by Satan and his kingdom serfs. We need to know how to fight in the Spirit while hanging on to Jesus, the author and finisher of our faith.[22] Man's intellect is highly regarded by some, but great as it is, it can not get us to heaven— only the belief in Jesus Christ as Lord and Savior can do that. The simple trusting faith required in the salvation work of Jesus is one of God's great mysteries.

Strieber mentions he had some "Out of Body" (OBE) Experiences. In *"Transformation,"* he relates that while at his cabin one afternoon, he was on the couch with his eyes closed. Though not asleep, he was carefully moving his attention from place to place over his body in order to strengthen his sensory awareness. This was something he had done for many years; a suspicious practice because of its Hindu origin. On this particular occasion, he had the strange sensation of hearing voices saying, "Oh, good, now we'll show you something."[23] He then appeared in two places at one time. One was where he had been resting on the couch, and the other place was in another location, engaged in another activity.

This was not the first Out-Of-Body (OBE) experience for him, and he felt no fear associated with the idea. He believes most people are afraid of Out-Of-Body experiences for the same reason they are afraid to explore reincarnation.[24] I hope all Christians fear dabbling in the OBE activity. Intelligent powers promote the adventure of OBE experiences because it somehow appeals to our curious desire for universal awareness, (a grab for deity), and a quest for adventure. Fowler, the author of "*The Watchers*," states that Out of Body Experiences (OBE) and Near Death Experiences (NDE) are similar.[25] He mentions that one (NDE) might initiate the other (OBE). He also suggests a possible connection between UFO's and OBE'S.[26] This could explain why people who have OBE experiences are candidates for alien encounters. Fowler is probably correct in drawing a connection between alien visitations and OBE/NDE. [27] (However, it is important to note that not all people who experience an OBE/NDE are abducted by aliens).

In both of Strieber's books, aliens claim they can recycle souls.[28] I believe this means they can move souls from one body to another. Nowhere in the Bible does God say He recycles souls, or for that matter has any need to recycle anything. If God has found no need to recycle fingerprints or DNA codes, it is highly unlikely there would be a need to recycle something as important as a soul. Could anything be more unique than the eternal human spirit? I believe it says that He creates, and destroys—*He does not recycle.*

The topic of Wicca, a form of witchcraft, came up in Strieber's experiences. However, according to him it was not related to Satanism and other such perversions.[29] I'm not sure how one comes to this conclusion, unless they think there is a difference between good evil, and bad evil.

Wicca, it seems, is based on ancient western Shamanism, which is considered to be one of the oldest of human religious traditions. It is very similar to native American and African religions that deal with a love for the earth.[30] Perhaps this is where we get the idea of a "living" earth. With this connection it seems that we have come full circle with the New Age movement promoting the "living earth" belief.

Wicca has seen a rebirth among New Age teachings. Occultic activities along with UFOs and alien visits seem to draw many individuals who are adrift without any solid religious direction in their lives. Perhaps this is the clue secular researchers have missed or ignored. A person with no solid religious direction in their life could be highly vulnerable to alien abductions and occultic experiences.

Strieber believes that whatever the visitors are, they have been responsible for paranormal phenomena ranging from the appearance of gods, angels, fairies, and ghosts, to the landing of UFOs's in the backyard of America. [31] I believe he is right, and yet, I don't think he fully comprehends the truth that all occultic activity (including Wicca), is part of Lucifer's plan to control man's ultimate destiny. Strange sightings like the

Sasquatch, Seti, and the Loch Ness monsters can be
added to the para-normal list because they all share the
same vanishing ability. These items like UFO's are all
elusive and may be connected to the same spiritual
mystery.

The author (Strieber) goes on to say something very
interesting which I quote, "It should not be forgotten
that the visitors...if I am right about them...represent
the most powerful of all forces acting in human culture. They may be extraterrestrials managing the evolution of the human mind."[32] What a chilling thought!
Again I ask, where is God in all of this? Did God take
down his "shingle" and go home? Without the teachings of Jesus and the Holy Spirit's counsel, we humans
are no match for super alien intelligence that can roam
the universe at will. But God has not left us alone! He
offers us protection that no force from the universe can
overcome, and that is Jesus and his shed blood.

Fallen Angels

Before Lucifer and his angels fell out of heavenly
grace, they must have had time to build a ruling structure (kingdom) of their own. God simply let them do it
to their ultimate end. The struggle of the alien kingdom is being played out in the lower heavens, and on
earth. Believers committed to God's son (Jesus), will
inherit the kingdom that God has prepared for them.
This inheritance is why I believe Lucifer hates man and
desires to use man to foul the plan of God. If this is
indeed the end of the age, is it any wonder about the
excess flurry of intelligent evil and extraterrestrial activity.

If we are to accept that aliens are real, then we must realize that in all probability we are dealing with fallen spirit beings in most, if not all cases. What they can tell us are wonderful lies, because they come from the author of all lies—Satan himself. What we should give the spirits in return is a bad time. The Bible tells us, "to submit to God, and resist the devil..."[33] and we can do that best by letting God inhabit our presence while we cling to Him, the creator of life. It is important to remain calm, and develop a stronger relationship with Jesus regardless of strange circumstances or alien endeavors.

The following statements are a summary of important revelations that can be deduced from the author's books *"Communion"* and *"Transformation."*

1. The aliens are real and physical. They also function on a non-physical plain.[34]
2. The aliens can enter the mind and affect or change our thoughts.[35]
3. The aliens have demonstrated that body and soul are separate entities.[36]
4. They claim to have the ability to move the soul in and out of the body.[37]
5. The earth is a school where souls evolve and grow.[38] (Which is Hinduism).

Strieber feels that if this relationship with the aliens is to proceed we must continue it by using the most powerful tool we have—an open, inquiring and educated mind, free from prejudices and preconceptions, and above all, free from fear.[39] That is a brave declaration, in light of the fact that fear overwhelmed him during his many encounters.

Fear is one of the reigning tools of Satan. Strieber does claim he got stronger when he had to face his fears.[40] This may be so, but what happens when a person faces the final and most horrendous fear—the loss of his soul and knowledge that there is no escape? How can any mortal deal with the idea that God is no more, and only hideous aliens exist? From Strieber's abduction descriptions, including dealing with fear and terror, it sounds like an extension of hell!

The open mind is indeed a powerful tool; this is precisely why we must carefully stand guard over it. Opening our minds to alien and dark demonic forces, would also allow them to twist and reshape our thinking for the possibility of fighting against God Himself, causing worldwide rebellion. This would cause us to be supporters of Lucifer and share his ultimate fate.

8

Collective Blindness

Mankind is collectively entering into a spiritual blindness concerning the truth. Deep and deeper he is falling into a dark hole of deception. The result of this blindness is not immediately perceived. However, the evidence of this spiritual problem is found in every day media events. While researching New Age materials significant facts emerge that support this idea. Much of the material seems to accomplish one or more of the following items:

1) Introduce man to a new spirituality, (one involving people with scientific credentials like mathematicians, physicists and astronomers).

2) Lead society away from the Biblical perspective of God.

3) Twist Biblical scriptures to support new meanings and interpretations never intended by God, or taught by the Christian community; like astrology or channeling as a gift from God.

4) Provide Humanistic solutions for life's problems.

5) Social ailments can be fixed with more government and more money.

6) A need for equity. Building a society for the benefit of all. A place that does not tolerate nationalism or fundamental religions.

7) Establish a coherent religion that includes salvation for everyone. A religion that is not exclusive like Christianity.

The design of the New Age is plain for those who have Godly discernment—and clouded for those who don't want to see the obvious. Born Again Christians are supposedly led by the Holy Spirit. If this is true for the Christian, then what spirit is leading the non-Christian? Assuming everyone is affected by one type of spiritual influence or another, it is reasonable to assume another spirit will influence those who are not under Godly influence? The Bible mentions that those who are rebellious to Biblical precepts will acquire a spiritual blindness to the teachings of God. This blindness will funnel them toward an alternative (ungodly) spiritual consciousness. Popular New Age ideas merge truth with subtle lies. Examples of these are as follows:

1. Live the golden rule.
2. Have a better image of yourself. ("You gotta love yourself before loving others.")
3. Be tolerant of all religions and people's value/belief systems.
4. There is no such thing as Hell.

Point #1 is proper. Most can understand the golden rule. Point two sounds good. We all want better self-image. But we must deal with sin and repentance first before we can truly achieve it. The third item is a dead give away of ungodliness. This is just what the enemy

want us to accept—to be tolerant of American liberal
ideas, such Eastern religious thought, abortion, alternative life styles, state control of children's lives and so
forth. The last item does away with hell, making it okay
to reason the absolute will of God away.

The UFO Assault

Adding to the confusion brought on by cosmic connections to the unknown, there is another assault to
contend with. One that introduces the mind of man to
UFO experiences. UFO stories continue to proliferate
across the world as if propelled by an explosion. If the
aliens have been around since ancient times, (as some
suggest), why are they now *allowing* themselves to be
discovered? Do we somehow fit into their current time
schedule for the next step they have planned for us
regarding our awareness of their existence? Have they
planned their introduction to our species all along?

The onset of modern UFO sightings began in earnest during the 1940's. Those who have seen space craft
or beings from outer space were largely ridiculed and
thought to be a bit "off." They were put down by the
media with the help of so-called experts and debunk-
ers. This discrediting process discouraged and impeded
early serious investigation. The delay served the aliens
very well, allowing them to make deeper inroads into
personal lives and society unhampered. Civilian UFO
research organizations have previously complained
about how they were invaded and manipulated by government shills to keep the alien story from being told.

In 1947 near Roswell, New Mexico, a farmer found
the wreckage of a flying craft (saucer) made of materials he had never seen before. When he reported the

incident to the US Army nearby, they initially admitted finding a crashed saucer. Later, a barrage of contemptuous denials by the government were released to "reassure" the public, no such thing had happened. To deal with this potentially serious world problem, a host of unrealistic explanations were offered over many years. The explanations ranged from weather (radar) balloons, swamp gas, stars to faked photography.

Discrediting UFO events and persons who observe them is still the most effective method to control the release of this information. Faked saucers and people having fun feeding this phenomenon with phony stories have not helped to clarify the situation. There are simply too many independent credible stories to brush them all aside.

While alien experiences are bizarre, scary and very strange by our living standards, they are impossible for many to accept. Hence, these events are put down just because they are not experienced by everyone, and don't fit our "normal" pattern of life. Besides, we as a society fear most things we don't understand and act irrationally toward things we can't explain. It is much easier to ridicule and make fun of things we don't understand. Perhaps fear of the unknown is the reason why solid reports and events, given by credible people are not believed.

Adding to society's blindness is a lack of consistent credible event reporting by the American news media. An example of media indifference was discussed one night on the Art Bell radio talk show by two UFO researchers April 16, 1995. The researchers discussed the 1995 Mexico City UFO sightings. They reported that inhabitants of Mexico city watched continuous UFO sightings for 17 hours during the 1995 solar eclipse. The UFOs were seen before the eclipse, during the eclipse and well after the eclipse was over. Mexico's news media gave wide coverage to the event. The natives took a casual approach to the sightings. The American news media did not carry the story, a mystery in itself.

9

Is There a Government Within the Government?

Could aliens, or controlled humans, be in the bureaucratic government? It is rumored that tangible alien visitation and craft evidence does exist, but is shrouded in a cloak of secrecy. Books such as "*Majestic*" (a novel of fact and fiction), "*Above Top Secret*," "*The UFO Report*," "*UFOs and Alien Presence-Six Viewpoints*," "*UFO Crash at Roswell*" and many others, strongly suggest that flying saucer and alien remains (dead and alive) have existed. These remains are alleged to be on various government bases in this country. There are also unconfirmed reports that humans and aliens are working together in underground installations. Assuming the above statements are true, then government involvement and deceptions (called secrecy) must be exposed for the benefit of mankind. Could there be a dark activity, within the government?

A segment of television's popular Unsolved Mysteries program, dealt with people living in the Gulf

Breeze, (Florida area), who had experienced strange sightings in the sky. The book, "*The Gulf Breeze Sightings*," outlines these incidents in detail. Government agents, after producing their credentials to these specific individuals warned them not to speak about their sightings and encounters. In some cases, the lives of the citizens were threatened. In one case, pictures of the saucers photographed by an observer were sought by government agents. It makes very little sense when the government refuses to acknowledge these events. Why spend a lot of time chasing down observers, threatening them to remain silent? Are we still the people of the government—or just the governed?

The Reader's Digest Book entitled, "*UFO: The Continuing Enigma*," addresses these intimidating government officials as the "Men in Black" (MIB). They appear on the scene as threatening figures to intimidate UFO witnesses. Here, the implication leads one to consider that aliens can and do take on human appearance. The Reader's Digest book suggests that MIB's often use a speaking style that doesn't fit today's vernacular. Oddly, their dress as well as their speech, seems to date back about twenty or thirty years in style.[1] I wonder if alien research of earthlings is quite up to date? Brad Steiger and his wife, in their book *The Rainbow Conspiracy*, talk about a person who went through some very threatening personal experiences from MIBs because of his knowledge on UFOs. The individual indicated that MIBs and UFOs come from a civilization that flourish secretly in some remote area of earth—possibly underground civilizations.[2] Timothy Good in "*Above Top*

Secret" also makes reference to the existence of MIB's.[3]

"Above Top Secret," a book filled with incredible UFO reports, has been criticized as being fabricated information. I made slow and careful scrutiny of this book's information. Although I can't validate everything, it seems to be a reasonable and credible piece of work. I base my judgment on one of the reports in this book that I have personally worked on. As an aerospace engineer working on the Boeing Minuteman Missile project in the mid 1960's, I was responsible for a project covered in that book. While researching this document, I was startled to read about an event concerning ten Minuteman missiles that were unexplainably knocked off alert (green status) at a Minuteman base. A UFO was reportedly seen hovering over the Minuteman Launch Control Facility. Originally when I was handed this project, I had not been informed of UFO involvement. It was my job to organize a scientific investigation team and dispatch them to the base to look for causes that might explain why the missiles were suddenly knocked off alert status—which is virtually impossible.

The team of scientists and engineers found nothing to explain the missile malfunctions. Later, when it was rumored that a UFO was involved, the work mysteriously stopped. The government directed that a final engineering report not be written or submitted concerning the event. In other words, just forget about it. All other projects required final reports to be submitted.

Even then, did the government already recognize the potential threat against our society? It makes one wonder. Who is really in charge of UFO policy?

Yet, another governmental possibility exists. Could officials in the government operate at such a high level of secrecy, that a virtual tight lid has been clamped on alien events? This can certainly be cause for speculation. As mentioned in the books, "*Above Top Secret,*" and "*The UFO Report,*" the government either cannot, or simply won't, adequately explain UFO incidents to the public. Perhaps they won't because they fear not being able to quell the curiosity, and the possible hysteria which might result from public reaction if the facts became known. It would be an embarrassment for the US government to acknowledge UFO existence without being able to ensure the average "John Doe" that all is safe and under control. Perhaps, with what the government knows about UFO's, they cannot ensure anyone's safety! This could be the case as already proven in many documented abductions, downed aircraft, and other reports found in "*Above Top Secret.*"

William Cooper, author of "*Behold a Pale Horse,*" makes a case for the existence of a secret government. Cooper, formerly in Naval Intelligence, reveals information going back to the president Truman era, when plans were laid to establish a super secret agency to deal with UFO's.[4] This is also alluded to elsewhere. According to Cooper, the agency evolved with so much secrecy that today, it is almost a government within itself.[5] He describes a chronological series of events showing how the super agency got it's start under the NSC (National Security Council) and eventually became the NSA

(National Security Agency).[6] It is possible that part of this agency's work was to keep the public ignorant, away from the hair raising information they had on UFO's, abductions, sightings, captured alien aircraft and alien bodies.

If Cooper is right, there seems to be an internal governmental fear that keeps this information under wraps. It would seem fear is what generates government policy concerning what this information could do to the average person's ability to cope. Or worse—it might even result in the collapse of society's structure as we know it. Eventually, we are all going to find out. Is there ever a good time for bad news? I believe this information will be forced out officially (as it has been unofficially) and when it does, the public will question the motive and credibility of our government's actions. Perhaps by then it won't matter anyway, if the timing of released information coincides with the establishment of an alien controlled world.

After reading many scenarios of a possible government cover up, I began to ask what could be so shocking, devastating or important about UFOs and aliens concerning our society? Again, I thought about what would cause the government to hold back on one of the greatest discoveries since God created man. Some writers hint that the government is now feeding society bits and pieces of alien—UFO information/dis-information to prepare us for some kind of major earth event.

Again, this statement prompts the question, "What information could possibly cause our global society and the basic structure of religion to disintegrate if this information became known?" You must agree, this is a most intriguing question. Is it possible that faith in God and in particular, Jesus Christ, could be shaken or even shattered by some kind of incredible information? What would Christianity do if it found itself in a serious credibility bind? To whom would the people turn, and from whom would they get their answers? Traditional religion is not prepared to deal with this shocking knowledge.

Now that I've asked the questions, I will attempt to answer them. As mentioned throughout this book, we must realize that a great plan of deception (The Luciferic Initiation) is being worked out here on earth. God will allow this deception because of the wickedness of mankind. God says about the end times that He will send a strong delusion upon mankind. If He says it will be strong, then you can be sure it will be just that. However, God always informs *His people* when some great event is to occur. This is no exception.

The best way for me to answer these questions is to take the reader on an adventure.

Suppose an evil alien command (forces on high) developed a significant plan of deception for earth. The plan was introduced to certain select leaders of this world. Let's also say that aliens came in their magnificent space ships and landed at a base where they were anticipated. Upon landing they met in secret with military and civilian leaders. One of the civilian leaders was a prominent representative of a large Christian Denomination. During the course of the meeting, the earth leaders were shown many spectacular wonders. One being a holographic representation of Jesus being crucified and dying on the cross. The   aliens, demonstrating their intellec-

tual and technological marvels (powers), were able
to convincingly suggest to the earth leaders (including the prominent church leader) that it was the alien
hierarchy that brought man to this world. They alone
invented God and religion to control man's development, environment and destiny—that it was the
aliens themselves who invented and inspired the
Bible. Jesus was their invention and it was all a ploy
to keep mankind under their managed care (something like an *HMO only a lot bigger).

The shock of meeting these overwhelming creatures, with their awesome demonstrations of miraculous power, so overwhelmed the earth leaders that
they were barely able to function. The impact of this
experience was personally devastating to the earth
leaders. Other Government officials witnessing the
event took control of the outcome and determined
that mankind could not be told the truth for fear of
world wide calamity. If society ever discovered the
significance of that event, it would shatter the social, economic, religious and philosophical fabric of
our world. This information could cause the collapse
of the governing world economic structure as it is
known. Understanding the death and chaos which
might occur, government officials put a lid on the
event and initially said nothing. The information was
then put under the highest possible security classifi-
cation. After swallowing the significance of this event
and other UFO/alien phenomenon for many years,
the agency began to slowly leak information and *dis-
information in an attempt to lessen confusion, as
well as the economic shock which would result when
these events start to occur.

If the scenario described above actually happened, at one point, we can easily understand the government's motives for denials and secrecy. We can also see the reason for ridicule and threats heaped on those who speak out when they relate information about UFOs and aliens. It must become very difficult for secret agencies to control, especially when many credible reports of personal encounters become public and the government continues to be ho-hum about it.

The brief scenario related above is my attempt to answer the question; What classified information might be so bad that it could trigger the collapse of our society? I built this scenario, giving serious thought to an event related by William Powell. In his controversial book, "Behold the Pale Horse," Powell relates a story along the lines described above.[7] Whether the story is true or false is not the issue. I do not desire to get into the specifics of his book or the scenario mentioned above. My object is to bring up the possible downstream effects on Christianity may suffer if such a thing did happen. An intelligent ungodly force with a sophisticated, convincing and overwhelming power display could introduce man to a whole new universe. We might not only become world citizens, (the current push) but galactic and universal citizens as well.

One has also to consider the effects that might occur from similar events. What would happen to the average Christian who has a weak or luke-warm tie to his church faith? I personally believe lukewarm Christians (in mass numbers) would instantly stray to whatever offered them security and the promise of social stability. I also believe that Satan plans something wonderful—something that appears to be good without the God of the Bible. With a shaken and demoralized worldly populace looking for a way out, Satan's plan just could work...*for a while.*

This strange event, or some other similar event of profound impact, might bring on the potential use of the mark of the beast (666) for those who accept the new world system. When this occurs, the majority of the population will turn away from their traditional faith in God, and embrace the new social, technological and a religious (politically correct) system. Many will simply not adhere to a faith in God after aliens have shattered it by their overwhelming and convincing miraculous power displays. (Revelation 13:2b-4, *"...and the dragon gave him his power and his throne and great authority. And I saw one of his heads as if it had been slain, and his fatal wound was healed. And the whole earth was amazed and followed after the beast."*). However, there will be some who remain faithful because they recognize the lie. It will be a time of great fear and *transformation* away from God. Paul, the Apostle, spoke of a great apostasy, and abandonment of the Lord before the end.

For Satan to sabotage man, (which is really his primary work), he will have to invent or establish an elaborate yet significant and believable charade. Something that will shake the basic foundation of this world and yet entice followers. Many possible scenarios might work. Scenarios that include one or more of the following events: invasion of aliens, collapse of society, earthquakes, scary or wondrous signs in the sky, economic collapse, loss of faith in the government, wars, huge natural disasters and/ or any combination of these things. By these kinds of situations, vulnerable world leaders are made ready to accept anyone who could supply answers to critical problems—hence, the arrival of the antichrist and his, (not so) secret government.

True believers, secure in a firm relationship with their God, (Jesus) will have discernment to see through this deception. They will be able to withstand the onslaught of the enemy and help others resist the magnetic marvels of Satan's kingdom. Perhaps this is where the elect will be seriously tested, as they resist the alien inspired government.

Some Christians believe they will not be here when this evil begins to pour out on the earth. They believe they will be taken out or raptured off the earth. I would like to believe this thought, however, I really can't say it will happen. All I know is that we are still here and everything seems to be getting worse each passing day. I worry about those who think they will escape the end time trials, especially if they find themselves still here when the real hardship, suffering and cunning break out. Will their faith endure when things don't happen as they were led to believe? Folks, it's time to walk close to Jesus and stay there...no matter what.

10

A Battle For Control

Hovering lights appeared over a rural property in western Washington state on two separate occasions. These lights fascinated Sue, a woman who lived there for some time.

I had a chance to talk with Sue, a Christian who lives far from city lights near the Cascade mountains. With no street lights to illuminate the dark night skies, you can imagine the vividness of faraway stars in such a setting. After hearing her describe these hovering lights, I could definitely see a correlation between her experience and other UFO encounters that I had read about.

The hovering lights were observed on two successive nights. The first night, she saw a large orange light dancing in and out of the clouds nearby. She was awed at the sight and could not keep her eyes off the intriguing spectacle. While watching this orange light phenomena, she called her teenage son to the side deck of the house where he confirmed the amazing sight. She was not afraid of this strange spectacle, and later dismissed it.

The next night, while alone in the house she had a different experience. Looking out an upstairs window, a green and blue light was glowing brightly from the top of one of the tall fir trees nearby. At the same time, smaller white lights were observed going to and from the blue light. Her comments are similar to others who have had personal encounters with UFO and alien visitors. Although she doesn't remember seeing or speaking with aliens, her comment was worth taking note of. She said, "the feeling she was left with, was like something had been taken from her—like she had been mentally raped." Drawn at first by curiosity, Sue's experiences resulted in a lingering fear of looking up into the night sky—as if something would be there, something she could not bear to see.

On that second night, while watching the lights in the top of the tree, her body shook with fear. An inner voice told her to turn away and not look. She believes the Holy Spirit was warning her not to look, however, her gaze became firmly fixed on the strange sight. The next day when she related the account to her family, her tale was not believed. On the same night, however flying saucers *were* reported in the vicinity of the mountains, not far from her home. Earlier in life, Sue dabbled in witchcraft, and that occult involvement may have resulted in her vulnerability to other spiritual experiences, like UFOs.

Some might think it was time to dig deeper into her experiences through hypnoses or regression therapy. I am not a believer in either of these methods and will discuss why in a later chapter. Since she did not recall any face-to-face alien encounter, I simply asked her to relate any other strange occurrences that she could remember.

Sue went on to describe a dream that seemed very real to her. (To fully appreciate it, the reader must know that Sue is an amateur artist, then actively engaged in taking art lessons.) At the beginning of her dream, she and her art instructor were talking outside the classroom. As she entered the classroom she saw a shocking sight. Manifestations of demons, were in the room and objects began to fly off the walls and off the desks. She heard what sounded like demons calling out to her. As she observed this bizarre sight, Sue was lifted off the floor and found herself floating near the ceiling. In her fright, she desperately wanted to call a Christian friend and ask for prayers. Instantly, a phone appeared in her hand and she was making the call.

As she continued to float near the ceiling, she watched helplessly as demons passed in and out through a soft spongy wall. Her exact words were, "they could go in and out through this soft spongy wall, at will." She recalls hearing a voice from within her saying, "This is wickedness at the highest level."

I believe her dream was a meaningful revelation; one demonstrating the use of extraordinary power to pass in and out of a human subject (the soft spongy wall) under demonic control. Control comes up time and again when dealing with demons, aliens and UFOs.

Sue is a sincere, Christian woman who believes and lives the salvation plan of Jesus. I know there are some who say that a Christian can not have occultic and strange things happen to them. My personal experience and research on these matters does not support that theory. As pointed out earlier, Sue may have unintentionally opened the door to her mind through past involvement in the occult. Sue's dream will take on additional meaning when compared to a similar experience found in the book *Encounters*.

A psychologist, using regression hypnosis, documented several cases of alien abductions which is covered in the book, *Encounters*. Of all the abductions described, one stands out prominently as a possible reason for alien visits.

This abduction began when a woman was taken aboard a saucer and came face to face with strange insect type beings. They wasted no time in assuring her that she would be all right. In spite of their assurance, she was terrified, finding she had no control over her body.[1] The flying saucer she was in made several stops as it traveled across the world and picked up people from different countries.

As they were picked up, they became immobilized like her and were transported to a larger mother ship.[2] In the larger ship, she saw human abductees lying motionless on a row of tables as they might appear in a morgue. As she was examined she was forced to endure several technical type procedures, some being very offensive. A specific event, (remembered with vivid detail), made her realize that aliens use human bodies, enabling them to exist in the physical.[3] This became apparent to her when she realized the aliens were able to draw power from her body. She suddenly knew it was energy they drew from her.

The battle for control of her body continued. When the aliens were in control, they entered and drew energy from her.[4] The process, as she understands it, is one of rejuvenation using the energy they obtain from humans for their existence [5] (perhaps for entering our dimension).

As described in Sue's story, this event also smacks of wickedness at the highest level. The procedure she endured definitely appears to be a spirit gaining possession and control of a person's body. When she was a young girl, she had inner strength to resist them. This made the aliens angry. A white light would appear that seemed to assure her she would be okay. The light gave her strength and ability to resist the aliens.[6] Perhaps the light represented God's protection when she was young and especially vulnerable. Later in life, she says the aliens were able to come in and out of her body at will, especially when she was off guard. This woman's frightening experience is similar to Sue's dream.

If these events actually happened, then one can conclude that UFOs, aliens and demon type activity can be combined in the same strange phenomena. It can also be deduced that aliens are becoming bolder and less inclined to hide themselves as they have in the past. This event demonstrates that aliens have made definite inroads into the physical and spiritual aspects of mankind.

Monster From the Sky

One dark evening (April 16, 1994), a young man, (eighteen years old), on his way home near Mt. Rainier in Washington state, had an encounter with a very strange looking animal. However, what he saw was more than just strange and more than just an animal.

An article came out in the Tacoma News Tribune, written by C.R. Roberts describing this young man's run-in with a bizarre sighting.[7] As the young man was driving home one night, his dash lights went out and his car came to an unexplainable stop. His head lights remained on and shone straight ahead to a scrubby clear-cut field. While wondering what was wrong he noticed what appeared to be feet coming down into the head lights in front of him. The feet were like a bird's with claws and all. It came down from above to land on a scrubby knoll about thirty feet ahead of his car. He saw feet followed by legs, then a torso with folded wings attached to the back of broad shoulders. The torso was followed by the head with tufted ears and a mouth with straight sharp teeth. The body was described as covered with blue tinted fur. The head looked like a wolf with yellow eyes.

The creature he later described, (a sketch was included in the article), could not be anything natural to our world. The young man indicated that it appeared to be about nine feet in height. The newspaper sketch of the animal looked like a medieval artist's rendition of a demon. See fig. 10-1 for a sketch by a local artist.

I believe this was a significant event, one that might help clear up the UFO/Alien mystery. I mention this because the description of what happened is not much different than if a UFO was present. In many close encounters, the car's ignition goes off, the engine dies, then the lights go out about the same time. In this case, the same thing happened with one notable exception. The vehicle dash light went out, but the headlights stayed on.

The newspaper account of the event leads me to wonder if the young man was "set up" by a higher power. This set-up appears to be a possibility from the young man's own words. His car stops unexpectedly without any reason. The headlights are perfectly in-line with the grassy clearing where the animal descends. The young man indicated the animal came down with a thud stirring up dust and just stood there, as if in a daze. After several minutes passed, the creature stretched out its huge wings (as wide as the road) and flew off in the direction of the mountain. The news article characterized the young man as an average high school senior who didn't drink, take drugs, play dungeons and dragons or listen to heavy metal rock music. He seemed to be a clean cut average guy—almost an unlikely person to be given this unusual event to witness. It is apparent that some higher power must have been in control of the event.

Comparing this event to a UFO appearance, one can draw certain parallels. Usually, UFO encounters seem to kill car engines, electrical systems, headlights and so forth. Now we have an encounter with a strange animal that looks like a demon and the effects are similar. Could UFOs, Sasquatch, Yeti, Loch Ness monster, and all other strange sightings come from the same trans-dimensional origin? After considering and evaluating this data for sometime, I have concluded, these strange apparitions could all be from to the same spiritual source.

Another reason I mention this is due to the comment made by researcher Linda Moulton Howe. On a radio talk show dealing with strange phenomena, she relates a possible connection between Big Foot and UFOs. She told of a farmer who saw and shot a Big Foot with a .30-06 rifle, only to have it instantly disappear in a flash of light. The occult world has always been replete with strange sightings that operate in the physical, as well as in the unseen spiritual realm. Another odd question about the monster that fell from the sky is, "why did the strange animal fly off and not challenge or engage the young man in any way?" In many instances,

UFO inhabitants engage humans through abduction, rides on UFOs and other frightening activity. The young man indicated no attempt was made to confront or threaten him in any way.

A few years ago, an evangelist, made a startling statement during a retreat I attended. He said, "As we come closer to the end times, demons will be cast down to earth more and more." I thought the statement was unusual, but like so many things we hear, I just filed the statement away in my memory. Yet, from the young man's description in the news article, it seems that is exactly what happened in this case—a demon literally fell out of the sky! He says, "The creature just stood there like it was resting; like it didn't know where it was or what to think of it's circumstances."

What are we to think? Was this demon cast down to earth? Was this event another warning to man, signifying that we are entering into the end time deceptions where the spiritual war will become more intense? Could UFO's be the culmination of what Jesus meant concerning the dragon and one third of the heavenly host to be cast down to earth? Is Satan's version about the end time, "a dressed up charade" concerning the fallen ones? It is very possible we are already witnessing end time difficulties. If so we are only be at the beginning of what we can expect the battle to be like. A challenge for us all.

Figure 10-1
Artist rendetion of the demon that fell from the sky.

11

What Aliens Say About God

This chapter contains information gleaned from published data about alien comments of God, even though I do not claim to be an expert on their perspective of God.

While browsing through many accounts of alien abductions, I noticed very few relevant comments concerning God. The few comments that were made are significant enough to make mention of.

Prior to the ground work laid for this book, I was convinced that Christians would never be subjected to alien visitations and strange UFO experiences. I have since changed my mind. The story of Sue, mentioned in the previous chapter, shattered my old myth. Additionally, there are other Christians who have undergone similar experiences.

One of these experiences has become quite notable. "The Betty Andresen affair" (referenced in the book, "*The Watchers*") was an event involving a professing Christian. It was difficult for me to accept and believe there were Christians who had undergone these experiences at the beginning of my research.

As I searched the Bible for explanation of these events, I found several Biblical passages that could be interpreted as UFO\alien type visits. Yet, God did not clearly point this out in his Word, and I wondered why. Perhaps, it was not His intention to make it clear because it was to be part of the massive end time deception—a test for all of mankind.

As we look into the alien perspective of God, it brings up a few interesting, if not chilling, prospects. In one case, an abductee asked the alien about God. The reply was they have God also, the same as ours, but there was no Jesus involved.[1] Is it possible Jesus exists only for us here on earth? I personally doubt this.

In another instance, the aliens talked about a *universal light* that exists for everyone—including the aliens. The light radiates out to all the planets in the universe and is a higher consciousness of thought, pure in every sense of the word. It is called "God" on this planet.

The aliens continued to explain that the light is in each of us. All we have to do is ask for it to awaken and grow.[2] Although this sounds innocent, it is tantamount to opening one's mind to the occult, leading to the maze of Lucifer's Initiation.

Aliens rarely speak of specific religions, only the universal light. Yet, in other cases, aliens appearing like "God-sent" helpers, (or angels), told abductees that they were here to change the world...to keep it from disaster.[3]

Apparently danger is imminent if the people on earth do not change the way they live. Presumably, they are here to help humans into a New Age of living and thinking, where future changes will be so powerful that only the strong will survive. They claim to be here in a capacity to give knowledge and understanding to the world of light, and to the children of God.[4]

The alien perspective of God, should provide a strong clue as to their motive. If they were created by the same God as ours, why don't they acknowledge Jesus? Jesus and God are inseparable for us here on earth, as we understand it in the Gospel of John and in many other Biblical passages.

I have grave doubts that the aliens worship our God. They may have been created by our Lord, but they certainly are no longer submitted to His "Lordship." First of all, the *universal light* is probably another reference to Lucifer (the bright *"star of the morning"*...Isaiah 14:12). The Apostle Paul, tells us that Satan can appear as an angel of light, and of course, the alien criterion for God does not match ours.

While it is true there is only one God of the universe—who will make all things subject to himself—it is also a Biblical truth that fallen heavenly hosts (fallen angels and demonic beings) follow after another god...Lucifer.

In many accounts, aliens appear to be imparting knowledge to us. Knowledge on many subjects including altered ideas about God. As for the knowledge they give us, I'm convinced it is a "superior" knowledge that is meant to slowly evolve mankind to be in accord with Lucifer's plan. That is, to make their god (Lucifer) our god.

This universal light is a unique deception also. It seems too good to be true. The following quote was taken from the book "*Encounters.*" It speaks of the universal light.

"We are here to change the world for a better development in the universe...to be closer...to surviving planets...in the nearby universe. We are here to give to all, new life, new force, a new being, an exciting, wonderful world of knowledge. Peace be with you forever and always."[5]

These comments become a very frightening set of words when examined closely. Notice, the aim is to improve the world...and us. New life? New force? New being? *Wonderful world of knowledge*?!!! Didn't Satan promise Eve that her eyes would be opened when she ate of the tree of the knowledge of good and evil? "Knowledge" is the key word. The exploitation of knowledge is "the plot" to entice man to receive, information not meant for us...Modified, controlling knowledge cloaked as a "whole new wonderful world of knowledge."

Notice also, their parting statement "Peace be with you." It sounds like someone is trying to imitate Jesus when He appeared to the apostles after the resurrection. This is clever and well thought out, but it has the earmarks of a deceiver behind it.

And what is the meaning of, "a new being, and a new life?" What happens to the one we have now? This begins to sound like Satan's version of the millennium.

Much of the published UFO\alien data suggests that they are a highly intelligent race of beings with a technological capability far in excess of anything we have on earth. Their ability to travel and make use of exotic materials makes that obvious. In the Book of Daniel (12:4), it says that in the end time knowledge and travel will greatly increase. Godly and ungodly knowledge, along with travel, have been on a rapid increase now for generations. Hence, today we have an explosion of information and technology which has accelerated within the last 100 years... (from cars to rocket ships, and from radios to the world wide web).

Our own knowledge and technology base is greater now than in any other similar period of our history. When you buy a computer for instance, you know that tomorrow will bring new and better ones into production, making yours obsolete. The same process is happening to most electronic items. With all this change, it is comforting to know that God does not change. He is the Beginning and the End, the First and the Last. Our faith is built on God's Word and not upon the whim of some alien culture, maneuvering mankind toward a new technology and strange, untrue revelations about God.

12

Theological Issues

The Christian church is poised at the edge of a long slide into spiritual deception. One that will supply no explanation for the trans-dimensional intelligent wave that is about to engulf it. In light of the spiritual theological ignorance concerning aliens for the church, Christians are just too busy shoring up their faith doctrines against each other (theological walls). The Church is blind to what is coming through their front doors. It is called the New Age doctrine.

These doctrines include many faces of humanism and liberation theology which have taken deep hold of the church scene. Truly it is evident that we are in the "Laodicean church age," found in the book of Revelation—meaning *"The sleeping church."*

An example of where the church is, (concerning the New Age) was brought to my attention by a local pastor. While discussing specific dangers of the New Age movement with this pastor, I was surprised when he made the comment, "the New Age is passé and dying out under its own weight." This unrealistic comment really grabbed my attention. With the obvious onslaught of the New Age making deep inroads in society, it's no longer a future threat that might happen—it has already happened and been integrated into the fabric, of our society as well as the church scene. The pastor's comment, is indicative of church's blindness concerning he New Age movement and its ultimate goal. I believe his attitude represents the average mentality found in the Christian body.

John Mack, M.D. who is professor of psychiatry at The Cambridge Hospital, Harvard Medical School, was asked a question during a radio interview pertaining to religion and the cases of abduction that he studied. He described one situation where a fundamentalist Christian originally thought aliens were demonic. The Fundamentalist later changed his mind after developing a relationship with these beings. He realized they were something else, although he was not sure what. The experience was different than what religious training had led him to believe. Mack further explained that no particular pattern of religious background is associated with the alien experience. He also indicated that these experiences take precedence over peoples religious backgrounds.[1]

Religion will struggle through a very difficult future if what the above mentioned Christian concludes is true. While religion did not prepare him for the encounters he went through, it does not necessarily mean there is a legitimate independent "space alien culture," apart from God either. Other dimensions, space beings, time travel and all that a person imagines, can still be used by a very astute adversary to convince man to think, there are other "life avenues," than the one Judeo/Christianity offers. Convincing the average earthling into believing that alien experiences take precedence over a persons religious background is the real trick. I don't believe even Dr. Mack grasps the depth of the deception he and his clients were wrapped up in. Alien experiences can take precedence over religion only if a person lets it. It is difficult for me to understand how a fundamentalist Christian could fall for alien deception.

Another shock for me was how an expert in the field of psychiatry, Dr. Mack, ends up explaining the role of religion from an abductee's point of view. It is as though alien experiences somehow over-ride religion. Something is wrong here. Since when did religion abdicate its role and give psychiatry authority to speak for religious faith? Where are the religious theologians who are able to explain to psychiatrists and others the meaning of these phenomena, and reveal it for what it is? Are there any?

When the Church finally wakes up, and realizes UFOs and aliens do in fact exist, they will be ill prepared to know how to deal with the challenge. The church has no clear Biblical basis on how to treat these phenomena. They will either say its from God or from Satan, but in a way that will sound religiously unacceptable to many. It will certainly pose an interesting problem for the church. The obvious question is, "What is their relationship to God?" How does Jesus and the Holy Spirit fit into the extraterrestrial scheme? It seems that psychiatrists, psychologists and hypnotists are now gaining an upper hand in explaining to church people what these things mean. What happened? Has the real world turned upside down?

Introducing a New God

New Age theological problems seem to sprout up from a variety of interesting issues. One problem can be seen from an article published in the Tacoma News Tribune on December 19, 1992.[2] According to the article, the Catholic Church and the Vatican are grappling with the possibility that other life forms exist in the universe. In the Spring of 1993, the Vatican began operating a large new telescope atop a 10,436 foot peak of Mount Graham in southeast Arizona (see Fig. 12-1). The plan is to locate planets in other star systems. It seems that the church is preparing to address the possibility of other intelligent life in the universe. The Church desires to ask other life forms about the Bible, Adam and Eve, original sin, and Jesus. Scripture does indicate that angels desire to know the mystery of Jesus and the cross (1 Peter 1:12). However, it does not say if they are good angels, or fallen angels who seek this understanding. Scientists using the Hubbell telescope have already discovered planets orbiting other nearby star systems; planets that might have a possible life support environment.

The problem with the church's approach is simply that it could backfire on people with good intentions. The worst case scenario might be once aliens are discovered on other planets and contact is made, they could manipulate mankind for their own selfish purposes. Some think this is already happening.

Imagine how convincing the aliens could be, with new revelations about the origin of the universe and the earth. At the same time they could show great wonders (like time travel and miracles), with the purpose to draw people away from their Bible-based faith, and introduce a more rational and complete faith. It could be a faith that introduces a new god of the universe—one we haven't thought of before. Surely it has the potential to lead many in the wrong direction and provide the building blocks for an alien-controlled world. How wonderful it will seem to those looking for the way to Nirvana, or some other ungodly Utopia. The horrendous shock would come of course once again, as in the garden of Eden when the participants discover they have been horribly deceived. It will be too late for those who must pay the price for ignoring the one true God and His Word.

This has all the earmarks of a very stealthy and overwhelming scheme that could just work, for a while. Then, as the real intentions are revealed it could become a bit scary for mankind, and possibly too late for those who buy into the "Big lie." I believe Satan's real motivation is to wonderfully stun, shock and seal the fate of many before they can resist. Certainly, this is not what Jesus offers to those who follow Him.

Here is another haunting question for the church to deal with: Is Jesus the Savior for those on other planets? Does the blood of Jesus extend to them for salvation as well? If so, how do other life forms come to know this? And who is supposed to tell them? Jesus left us with instructions concerning the earth, but He never said anything requiring man to expand the work of salvation through out the rest of the universe. It would seem a bit presumptuous for man (in his limited ability to travel in inter-galactic circles), to assume this role. I believe if the message of Jesus and the cross are meant for other planets, then God will provide the messengers.

Many Christians are getting into the act of wanting to believe in the good nature of space aliens. They are inviting them to make themselves known. Another news article showed a photo of a Texan standing in the middle of a $10,000.00 UFO landing pad he had built in a gravel pit.[3] His idea was to invite a UFO to land and make themselves at home. The landing pad had a message stenciled across it in large letters that welcomed the aliens, and the Lord Jesus! He obviously wanted to cover all bases. (see Fig. 12-2). At first, I thought this was amusing. However, I began to wonder if we are being conditioned to think this way. Could aliens be working to instill in us an unconscious desire to invite them to earth? Is their real plan a set-up, getting us to invite them to come in all their glory? Is our quest to know them a fatal quest?

If galactic citizens do exist, they provide many theological problems. For instance, one could ask: "If God is in charge of creation, then why are strange beings from space (or who knows from where) allowed to access and control human beings openly and freely?" From many accounts researched, aliens operate with impunity, doing whatever they wish with human abductees. Some authors indicate, lives have been lost and persons have been known to disappear permanently. Do they have this kind of power over humans? Does our God allow this? Is there a set of celestial rules or guidelines that aliens operate by— unknown to man? These questions do not have an absolute answer—at least not yet.

Over the years, Christians have learned to be aware of negative (demonic forces) influences that affect humans. The Bible supports and discusses these influences in detail. For example: Satan's temptations offered to Jesus in the desert represent one set of evil

influences. Jesus casting demons out from those afflicted by them is another account. These Biblical instances represent no new surprises. However, the challenge for Christians nowadays seem to be wrapped up
in the occult, as well as the appearance of aliens and
strange beings which the church has had no consistent
viable answer, other than to say, "they are evil."

Are these influences new or are they old? Are they
inter-dimensional? Have they been here all the time?
Are they just now in the process of revealing themselves
as part of the end time deception? In some abduction
accounts aliens say they act as caretakers over the earth
and are going to change man's social, religious, and technological structure. This is a mouth full. Where do they
get the authority to say this?

Space traveling aliens appearing as rational,
beneficient God-sent Helpers, presents another church-
related issue. Just who are these Helpers and Guardians that plan to lead man into this *"Age of Enlightenment,"* by sharing great breakthroughs in a spiritual technology that expands their interpretation of, "The good
life?" This is sometimes referred to as the paradigm
shift by New Agers; A shift into a New Age of consciousness for man. There are many books available that discuss this shift, but I believe they all result from the
spirit of the anti-christ.

If this becomes the case, the church will have a great
battle on its hands just understanding what is happening. In the process, there will be such a profound religious confusion, (unlike anything previously encountered among church leaders) and Christianity could
suffer significantly. Other religions will not fare any
better. If leaders of the Christian church are not in tune
with the Holy Spirit, walking closely with Jesus when

all this occurs, they will not be able to deal with these false wonders. Many will fall. It is time for pastors to look beyond the collection plate and seriously prepare their flock for the spiritual battle already on the way.

The Light

Numerous personal experiences concerning "*The Light*" abound, and continue to proliferate. A "light" experience is often assumed to be a God experience. This is not always true: In fact, it may rarely be true at all. The apostle Paul addresses this in the book of Galatians, where he says, Satan can appear as an Angel of light. Many reported Light visions result from out of body (OBE) and near death experiences (NDE) with brilliant, colorful, incredible and overpowering displays of the hereafter.

Awe inspired experiences might explain why a person can be swept away, believing that God was part of it. A visit to the average retail book store will produce many books with titles encompassing the word, "Light." Some examples are: *Closer to the Light, Embraced by the Light, Transformed by the Light, Beyond the Light, and Saved by the Light,* just to mention a few.

People desperately looking for answers to life, and people trying to find a way out of complex problems, are ripe to accept what ever appears to be Godly. Unfortunately, they are also ripe to accept a counterfeit god in the process. The strength of New Age spirituality can be evidenced by the popular acceptance of these "Light" books. Awe inspiring experiences tease a person into believing there is another road to heaven. A road that reveals wonderful mysteries like psychic OBE/

NDE experiences, astral travel, visiting exotic places with huge crystal cities and so forth. All "Light" experiences should be viewed with extreme caution because as they tend to mix traditional Christianity beliefs with New Age meditation and the occult.

I equate *light phenomena* experiences as similar, or the same, as those who have claimed to have been abducted by UFOs. A few of these abductees tell a compelling story and sound almost giddy about how they have been abducted hundreds of times. After listening to these people on various shows, I have concluded that since they have accepted the fact about being abducted, as well as physically modified through implants...their stories are no longer credible about what happened. The reason I say this is because they have bought the lie. These abductees feel that they now understand about being a part of the great awareness of some universal cosmic consciousness. Its a consciousness that talks about a creator and a grand plan. They believe they are now privileged to show man how he is to fit into this universal plan. These people talk of a God, but again it does not line up with the Bible or a Godly awareness of Biblical values except in some general way. The reason this becomes a serious concern is because they sound so good, and have the ability to influence others to buy into the deception. The *"light"* experiences likewise have a similar affect.

An article in a national tabloid highlights man's gullibility in believing there is "someone out there" with a better religion. The tabloid published a two page article in May, 1994 explaining how God sent aliens (angels) to create the world.[4] It went on to explain that all the miracles and great stories in the Bible were due to the intervention of aliens and space ships. Although these claims may be funny to some, the stories serve a purpose in preparing man for the advent of aliens and the new religion they are forging. Perhaps its already too late for the church to take action in order to get on top of this mystery.

Apparitions and Visitations

Angelic apparitions and visitations continue to be a serious spiritual problem. Visits from supernatural beings have been clever enough, to fool many religious people. Some apparitions come looking like glowing saints of old, or as bright heavenly entities. Appearances from celestial beings, should not automatically be considered as a good event. They may not be from God at all, and must be examined closely by what is revealed.

While scripture speaks of God sending angelic messengers to man, we must always be aware of the counterfeit messengers that Satan, the great deceiver, sends our way. All apparitions and their messages must be questioned in the light of God's written Word. Many sincere Christians have been led astray by a clever adversary. In my experience, I have seen good people with honorable intentions fall for clever frauds. While religious training and age old tradition preserves the way of doctrine, it fails woefully when used to discern spiritual activity. Religious tradition can change and therefore be open to heresy—i.e., embrace beliefs counter to Biblical scripture. God given discernment will alert one to potential pitfalls if they are grounded on scriptural truth.

As covered previously, aliens indicate they are poised to change our society for our own good. I believe this translates as a conscious effort by spiritual beings to change the tenets of Christianity, elevating Satan into a force of good, and simultaneously making Jesus and God of the Bible obsolete. The trappings of ungodly but pleasant sounding wisdom, coupled with awesome wonders, is simply bait to hook man into believing them.

This may sound extreme, but there is no other rational explanation for the Christian. The deception is so clever, and appears so "right," that many will believe the signs and wonders of the Antichrist and follow after him. While pondering how some of these deceptions might occur, an interesting event took place with a close Christian friend who nearly bought into one of these schemes. This friend gave me a video cassette featuring a woman who had visitations from an angel, Jesus and the Father. Although the video was provided with good intentions, and the message was touted as a Godly event, I was shocked when I viewed it, and realized it was promoted by members, of a large denomination. The person who nearly fell for the deception has a precious heart, with a love for her faith. She also has a strong personal relationship with Jesus.

The video portrays a very warm and charming woman telling about an angel that began to visit and "teach" her of spiritual matters. Soon she was visited by Jesus and the Father. She related how Jesus would take control of her hand and write answers to questions that she would ask. Her hand would automatically move and write the answers. This dictation varied from a short period of time to many long hours. The context of the message was very "religious," using a specific language and terms that their major denomination could easily recognize. The message, though considered good by religious standards, was seriously flawed and would not hold up to Biblical scrutiny.

The real issue is not the flawed messages, but the New Age technique used to deliver the message. It is known as *automatic writing, an old trick of the occult, not much different from the infamous Ouija board.

This woman described many events that she went through. One particular event jumped out as obviously suspect and manipulative. She claimed during a visit from the Father, that she had to recite the Lord's Prayer over and over for thirteen hours. She did this because she just, "couldn't get it right."

This technique was a manipulative method used to get her to say a "mantra" (chant), an eastern mystic technique, for a spiritual entity to gain control over a person. All this was done using the Lord's prayer. Similar events have been described in the book, "*The Beautiful Side of Evil,*" by author Johanna Micheleson. That author, described how the Lord's prayer was spoken while psychic surgery was being performed. In that case, they were encouraged, by the channel spirit, to say the Lord's prayer! It's not hard to see how evil spirits can use even the Lords prayer for the wrong reasons. Truly an abomination!

It seems we as Christians have to learn over and over, the lessons of the Bible. What if the Bible and its instructions are no longer followed in the future? Godly discernment is essential if we are going to avoid being led into the New Age through the veil of phony religious, and so-called *holy messages*. An obvious aggravation concerning this apparition is the apparent ignorance of the church members, who supported and promoted an occultic entrance into the church. Not many

years ago the church took a strong position against the
occult and its practice. Now due to the influx of the
New Age, some look up their daily horoscope!

The power and influence of false apparitions and
visitations should not be under estimated. If alien powers on high can appear and disappear, abduct humans
and demonstrate telepathic communication, they must
be masters over energy and power sources we do not
understand. We come across as weak and vulnerable in
comparison to their technical abilities. Spiritual entities can produce many different types of apparitions,
ranging from gnomes, fairies, leprechauns, visions of
saints or great historical personalities. Satan in his role
of as an "angel of light" becomes a very distinct adversary. Some religious folk, for instance, will follow visions
of Mary. Others might follow a great saint or another
entity. God can certainly send any messenger He wants,
however the source of all visions must be tested. This
is done simply by listening to what is said by any apparition, and testing it against God's Word. Some definitely fail the test. Far too many, want to believe everything appearing supernatural, as helpers sent by God,
especially if it has a religious tone to it.

Ben Alexander, a former psychic and occult medium,
explained how energies are taken from people to produce the strange visual apparitions that entice so many
occultic followers. In his book, *"Out From Darkness,"* he
relates some of the occultic evil practices he was involved in before, and how Jesus set him free to serve
the one True Living God. He describes the energy vibration many seem to be caught up in as follows:

*"Many strange things took place in the seance room. Often it
would feel cold to us. I later learned that this was because ecto-*

plasm was being taken from us in order for the spirits to solidify. Satan uses a life force that God has given us to work his counterfeit signs and wonders."[5]

He further quotes Paul of the Bible saying;

"*The coming of the lawless one will be in accordance with the work of Satan displayed in all kinds of counterfeit miracles, signs, and wonders, and in every sort of evil that deceives those who are perishing. They perish because they refuse to love the truth and to be saved. For this reason God sends them a powerful delusion so that they will believe the lie.*"[6]

During another seance experience, the author revealed the focus of the evil spirit's effort. The spirits said, "*In the spirit world we work on pure thought. When we can take control of your thought we can easily take control of your mind and then use your brain to relate our thoughts to people.*"[7]

(From this revelation it's easy to see why a person must guard their mind and not play with the occult. No matter how a person perceives the occult and its many forms, its purpose is meant to deceive the players and ultimately destroy them.)

The above comments from an ex-occult medium is also supported by a great man of God, Smith Wigglesworth, who lived in the late 1880's through the early 1900's. Smith indicated that if the devil can capture a person's thought life, he has won a mighty victory over that person.

He also said that it is Satan's business to inject thoughts into human minds. This is further evidence indicating that the mind is the real battleground. Why would aliens, demons and other entities be so concerned about the mind and spirit of man, unless they are the places where the enemy either wins or loses?

Generational Curse

The Christian community has recognized that curses can go back several generations. The Bible says so. Typically, people who dabble in witchcraft or other forbidden practices bring curses into their lives. People under a curse who died in an unrepentant state would hand the curse down from generation to generation, until the cycle was broken by a person renouncing the evil practice. This is nothing new to the average Christian: Yet, many (including Christians) may be afflicted by curses they are ignorant of; ones that go back many years through family roots.

I believe that curses rooted in the past, can be an enabling mechanism for strange occurrences. ESP abilities, channeling, various obsessions, alien visitations, demon possession and some apparitions all could be manifestations resulting from curses. This might be the reason why entire families experiencing UFO phenomena go back many generations with it.

For a long time, I wondered if there was a connection between a generational curse and a UFO/alien confrontation. In other words, can a curse be an open door, making a person susceptible to occult activity—including UFOs and aliens? If this is possible, then perhaps curses are the root of personal chronic problems, which cause various hindrances in the lives of people.

In Raymond Fowler's book, *"The Watchers,"* he mentions what appears to be a spiritual pattern (generational curse) with families experiencing UFOs. He uncovered a pattern, that indicates aliens visited persons of a particular family for several generations.[8] Generational curses are not new or radical ideas. They began in the garden of Eden (original sin) with the fall of Adam. We all labor under that particular curse until set free by the blood of Jesus.

Researcher Linda Moulton Howe, introduced another mystery for the church to deal with. During an interview, she was asked for an answer regarding "the possibility of a grand impending introduction of awareness concerning our place in the cosmos." Linda mentioned that her visit to a base in New Mexico (Kirtland Air Force Base near Albuquerque) resulted in being shown data about the U.S. Government's retrieval of a saucer and alien bodies. She was also shown data suggesting alien "*grays" were involved in genetic manipulation of primates on earth, making them responsible for the Cro-Magnon Man development.[9]

This issue was also raised by Fowler, the author of *The Watchers*. He discussed the findings of Pierre Teilhard de Chardin, (a priest at the Catholic Institute in Paris) a noted Paleontologist. At issue for Chardin was the large gap between Neanderthal Man and Cro-Magnon Man. There didn't seem to be a link between the two ancient developments of man. Fowler asks the question, "was Cro-Magnon Man placed on earth intact or was he the result of Neanderthal Man? (by genetic manipulation).

He goes on to say, "if either case were true, it would go a long way in explaining the genetic connection manifested in UFO abduction reports."[10]

If what these people say is true, then who knows what the future holds for mankind? These questions come to my mind, "Is this what the aliens want us to believe? That they created man? Is this their attempt to discredit God as the Creator?" This line of reasoning ultimately leads to the follow-up question, "Who needs God?"

One can see what a massive plan this becomes, i.e., replacing God with technical and spiritual wizards who are vastly superior to humans, and leading mankind into the New Age of modified life and fulfillment. What a thrill it must be for those who think they can rebel against God, and replace Him with a lie and yet embrace it as truth. In the midst of their folly, one can only imagine the calamity that will befall them when their "truth" eventually fails to shore up their beliefs...

Linda Moulton Howe is well known for her work on *animal mutilations and crop circles. Her research is considered to be of the highest professional and credible scientific work. Documented findings of her work is covered in her book, *"Alien Harvest."*

The Clash of Spirituality

There is a definite line drawn in the sand between New Age spirituality and traditional Christian spirituality. A war brewing from ancient times will eventually culminate into a giant clash between God and Satan. Recruits are being drawn in and trained to fight on both sides. The out come is already revealed in the Book of Revelation in the Holy Bible. However, many recruits of the Luciferic Initiation are not aware that they are being prepared to fight God, making them doomed already. An example of this struggle can be found in the book, *"The Celestine Prophecy."*

Many positive comments are attributed to this popular New Age book. The author, James Redfield, creates an adventure about a secret manuscript found in the Peruvian mountains. The book covers an American man's day to day adventure with various people who cross his path, all in search of the various insights found in the secret manuscript. The manuscript explains the meaning of life with a new spiritual consciousness that will be made available at the end of the second millennium, (just prior to the year 2000).

The *"Celestine Prophecy"* is a book that teases the mind. It will prepare many to delve into life insights and the coming consciousness wave. The manner in which the material is presented gives simple answers concerning man's evolution and what he is to accomplish while on earth—certainly something many are searching for. On the surface, it satisfies man's quest for meaning, and at the same time connects his spirituality with the cosmos (the entire universe). The book has a ring of truth and a form of godliness, offering participants a chance to plug into higher level energies from a source somewhere in the universe.

The author uses the Catholic hierarchy in Peru (as the bad guys), to keep the manuscript from being divulged. Manuscript revelations are depicted as a threat to traditional Christianity, causing the church to fight against divulging the information. The church has a problem with the manuscript because the source of the manuscript is unknown. In addition, it merges the New Age spiritual principles with Christianity for the express purpose of creating a more complete meaning to Christianity.

There have been many attempts to merge higher levels of occultic practices with Christianity, which is an obvious incompatibility. I consider this book perilous to the minds of people who read it as a guide to a better life. It typifies corrosive New Age theologies and raises man toward a divine nature.

The battle for man's mind is occurring between two different levels of consciousness. One is the God consciousness, acquired after a person makes a commitment to Jesus as Lord and Savior. The other deals with an altered state, which is usually referred to as achieving unity or oneness with the universe. This is the Lucifer consciousness. The battle is not over territory alone, but over the souls of Man. The entire heavenly battle extends down to earth. Christians afraid of the New Age, fail to realize that they are also called to a consciousness through Jesus Christ. This is sometimes referred to an obedience or loyalty to God. The God consciousness is not to be mistaken for New Age terms that refer to other christs or a "*christ consciousness." The enemy has set up a smoke screen for those who are weak in their faith and are able to be enticed to believe that Satan is God. The heavenly battle appears to be fought on three fronts; in heaven, in the minds of people, and on earth in both the physical and spiritual plains. Without Jesus leading individuals in their daily lives, there isn't much chance of them being victorious the end.

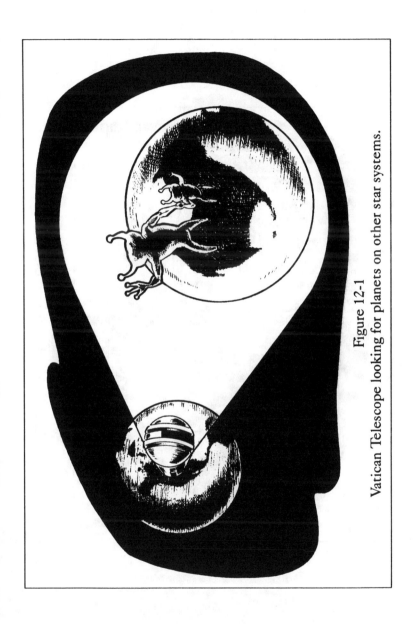

Figure 12-1

Vatican Telescope looking for planets on other star systems.

Figure 12-2
Texan inviting UFO's and Jesus Christ

13
Credibility

Are these so-called alien adventures real? Are the people involved in these encounters reliable? Is there such a thing as an unseen world? These, and many other related questions continue to plague the unbeliever.

The unseen world is believable for most Christians because the Bible reveals it's existence. In addition, many have experienced God and the Holy Spirit to some degree or another. Whether through a miracle, a healed marriage, deliverance, or a life made whole—they *know* God is real. Their faith brought them closer to God. Believing in something beyond the power of explanation, is normal for Christians. It is a way of life for them.

There is a huge chasm, however, between faith in God (and His unseen kingdom) and what is being revealed through other spiritual powers.

The subject of hypnosis is a good place to begin when talking about credibility. Many alien abductions are revealed through hypnosis. In addition, many events are uncovered through regression therapy. In fact, UFO researchers often use hypnosis to surface repressed events resulting from alien experiences.

Although hypnosis is somewhat acceptable in today's society, it wasn't many years ago when it was regarded suspiciously. Hypnosis was thought to be an amusing gimmick used in theater entertainment. Since then, its use as a tool has grown, gaining respectability among New Agers and psychologists alike who utilize it in their research of past life and event therapy. Many Bible believing Christians, however, have a problem with hypnosis because it leaves too many unanswered questions. Here are just a few:

1. Is hypnosis reliable?
2. Does the subject reveal their true subconscious nature?
3. Are they reporting on real experiences?
4. Is the subject in control of their own mind?
5. Does hypnosis lead to truth or fabrication?
6. Are the subjects being led by suggestion?
7. Who is in control of the subject under hypnosis?
   a. the person under hypnosis?
   b. the therapist?
   c. some other power or intelligence?

In Webster's II, (New Riverside Dictionary), the definition for hypnosis is:
"An induced sleep-like state in which the subject readily accepts the hypnotist's suggestions."

If a subject under hypnosis could readily accept the suggestions of a therapist, what unseen powers of intelligence, could also be making "suggestions" into their minds when hypnotized as well? Could Hypnosis be a type of trance or channeling? If so, who is in control of the revealed information, and where does it come from? (See figure 13-1).

Most likely hypnosis is highly unreliable when used as an avenue for revealing repressed events.

Regression therapy falls into the same bucket. Hypnosis needs to be investigated thoroughly in order to prove its credibility. That has not been done. In the book *"Transformation,"* author Whitley Strieber came to a point where he questioned the continued usefulness of additional hypnosis sessions.[1] There have been others who have underwent it and later questioned its credibility.

Man desperately needs to discern what real or subliminal power is in control of hypnosis sessions. One thing is for certain—the practice of hypnosis is growing in popularity and there are many who now claim to be hypnosis therapists. Many people are flocking to these therapists, looking for help. What they may be receiving, is a curse instead of help, by allowing their God-given spirituality to be corrupted by other spiritual influences. The lack of any governing agency, performance standard, or responsible overseer for these therapists is a major concern.

Is it possible that demon/alien beings, who seem to thrive on interfering with man's mind, have found a bonanza in hypnosis? In the book *Encounters*, one of the abductees said, "Through the mind. They (aliens-emphasis mine) can reach you".[2] In *"Communion,"* the author suggests visitors are entering our brains and our minds and we do not know what they are doing to us.[3]

Under these circumstances, the victim would recall the experience as real, even though it never actually happened. A person would be hard pressed to deny the event ever happened. In *"Communion,"* Strieber makes a few statements that might bear this out. He says:

"I would not be at all surprised if the visitors are real and are slowly coming into contact with us according to an agenda of their own devising, which proceeds as human understanding increases. If they are not from our universe it could be necessary for us to understand them before they can emerge into our reality. In our universe, their reality may depend on our belief. Thus the corridor into our world could be through our own minds."[4]

(In the past few years, tests have been conducted in regards to credibility of hypnosis with alien beings. The researchers gathered people together who had no prior knowledge or experience, or contact with aliens. Under hypnosis, the researchers asked them to imagine what it would be like to be abducted by aliens. These subjects amazingly imagined very similar scenarios as those who claimed to be actually abducted. This clearly shows evidence that the imaginations of people can be easily manipulated through hypnosis.)

Much has to be done to ferret out the truth behind hypnosis therapy. Secular psychologists, psychiatrists and para-psychologists should not be confidently trusted to do this alone, no matter how good their credentials are. The quality of people in these professions swing far and wide. A combination of qualified people working together with other objective, stable researchers, grounded in Judeo/Christian principles would definitely help. Anything less would bring on more suspicious and possibly tainted study results. Too many researchers have bits and pieces of what's going on, and their conclusions might be skewed. This is not to discredit the honest effort of those trying to find the truth about the UFO/alien enigma. A "central national depository," where data would be made available for research, would be a step in the right direction. The data could be evaluated by competent research teams to determine what this phenomena is all about. Controlled credible study results then could be released to the public, revealing the truth and perhaps embarrassing those hiding known facts into the limelight.

John Mack, a professor of Psychiatry at Cambridge Hospital (part of the Harvard Medical School) and a Pulitzer prize-winner, went out on a limb in 1994, when he published his findings in a book called, "*Abduction.*"

He treated about ninety different people who had alien abduction experiences. After trying to treat them, he found he had no answers for their condition. His dilemma was, what to do. He agreed, the source of the alien experience remained a mystery. I think, he was wrestling with the idea, there may not be a rational explanation for these experiences.

His training, experience and background did not prevent full blown criticism from his colleagues. Mack apparently was shocked at "the vehemence with which the faith" of mainstream scientific belief is being guarded.

Mack was warned by his colleagues not to take this alien stuff too seriously, or people would ridicule him. His experience highlights my point that no single authority can make sense out of these strange, yet spiritual occurrences. What he did was brave, boldly stepping out and telling the world what he thought, even though it brought him severe criticism.

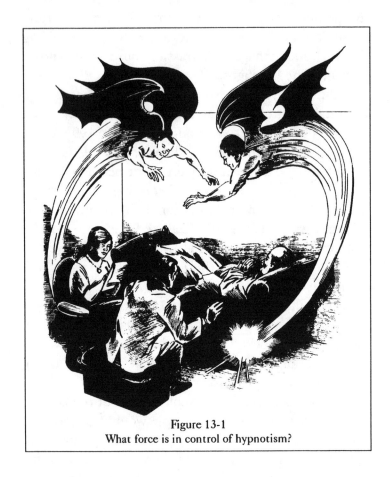

Figure 13-1
What force is in control of hypnotism?

14

Awareness and Protection

In a nutshell, apart from what God has given us, alien "space magic" should not be used as a guiding light for our development. Most people who distrust things they don't understand should not set themselves up to trust anything as enigmatic as aliens, or fairies and leprechauns.

Everyone in society has a collective responsibility to investigate reports of alien visits, and evaluate what they might mean. Whatever potential threat exists for the Christian, it represents double and triple jeopardy for the unbeliever. Although credible researchers are evaluating the staggering increase of extraterrestrial reports, there must be guarded skepticism towards the results. In addition, the lives of abductees need to be studied and evaluated to determine what type of background they come from. Questions concerning their religious, and possible past psychic or occult involvement needs to be addressed. This will determine the type of person having these experiences. Their lives have to be evaluated in order to ascertain what kind of spiritual fruit come from their lives. This is necessary, as part of an authentication process concerning all abductees and witnesses of these events. We may be dealing with people who have simply been spiritually duped. Our perception of alien technology and their sleuthing abilities, seem to breed a spiritual hunger for adventure. An adventure that is intriguing, which leaves open the possibility of experiencing a tantalizing physical and spiritual mystery. The alien ability to exist in a *trans-dimensional state, is not understood. For this reason it's highly probable that we are dealing with a sophisticated hierarchy, a higher order of evil, rather than standard demons.

Raymond Fowler in, *"The Watchers,"* quotes what aliens told Betty Andreasson (an abductee), that "their *technology* has to do with the spirit".[1] We live in a society where only religion and the occult truly deal with the spirit. Our secular, materialistic society (including science) does not normally deal with spiritual endeavors, because spiritual data cannot be gathered or measured the same way as scientific data.

If this country came under attack from a visible army, our society would respond. Yet, we seem to be helpless against the unseen spiritual reality assaulting society. The attack, however, may be more real than an attack from a physical army....and the consequences more devastating.

General MacArthur made two interesting comments concerning future enemies from space. On October 9, 1955 he issued a warning to the nations of the world that they had no choice other than to unite. As quoted in the New York times, MacArthur expressed his sincere opinion that the nations of

Earth must soon "make a common front against attack by people from other planets." He warned. "The next war will be an interplanetary one." In 1962, while addressing the graduating class at West Point, he stated: "We deal now not with things of this world alone. We now deal with the ultimate conflict between a united human race and the sinister forces of some other planetary galaxy."[2]

One thought which kept coming back to me while reading through many alien encounters and reports, is a comment made by Strieber in *"Communion."* He said, "there may be something far worse than physical death."[3] I can think of something far worse—the eternal loss of a person's soul/spiritual identity that unites them to God!

Para-normal and strange events should be a current top priority church study, testing them against God's written Word. The recent deluge of mysterious visitations and abductions represent a relatively new element not previously known to man. Is the world secretly being transformed to receive the *source* of all these strange intelligent beings? Are we being prepared for the final Anti-christ?

Remote Viewing

In 1995, US Central Intelligence Agency (CIA) officials admitted their involvement in a psychic activity termed *"*Remote Viewing."* Several psychics were employed for a period of 20 years. That is a long time for the government to experiment with these people. (It was rumored they were used to locate Sadam Hussein during Desert Storm, and obviously didn't work. He was never located until the war was over.)

It is a scary thing to realize that agencies of our government are now dabbling with dark powers. How many other dark collaborations are going on? Talk about credibility! On one hand the government treats UFOs as non-existent. On the other hand, they employ psychics as remote viewers. The time has come to put a stop to bland explanations, ridicule, and insults. Ridicule, which was effective for a short while, is no longer valid as it makes our government look like part of a conspiracy. While ignorance has never been an excuse to not obey the law, neither should it be an excuse to entrap us with things we not understand. Especially if these strange events can impact our lives, and ultimately alter or destroy us.

Protection

Is there protection against the Luciferic Initiation, and extraterrestrials who are invading our society? There doesn't seem to be if you believe the stories of personal encounters. Humiliated abductees were stripped naked and had to undergo examinations of their sexual organs, eyes, and teeth—and they had no say-so in these procedures.

Visible marks were left on arms, abdomens, and legs. Some females were forced to give up their reproductive eggs. Some males had to give up their sperm. In several particularly cruel incidents, females were forced to relinquish their unborn fetuses. There is no Biblical evidence indicating that God would do such things. This activity points directly to an ungodly hand at work.

How do we protect ourselves from this potent alien adversary? There is no easy answer that can be given from a worldly perspective. Any answer would be inadequate, since humans appear weaker and more vulnerable than we care to admit. Our collective intelligence does not begin to know how to handle this kind of overwhelming technical mastery.

Jesus is the only safe refuge in the universe. He not only saw the dilemma created by Satan from a heavenly perspective, but is the only One who could and did execute a plan to break the curse of creation gone awry. (see Fig. 14-1).

Belief in Jesus and the inspired Word of God provides the only hope and protection that aliens will not prevail against us. Even then, it is not that they won't try, because the prince of this world (Satan), is still running things. Jesus has already done the fighting for us and won the battle. Now, it is up to us, to take charge of our lives through that commitment to Him, and forsake any other belief.

From the Bible we learn protection is in the name of Jesus. In all the stories concerning the abductees, it is surprising how little most of them knew about the Bible, or Jesus. A person's vulnerability might be tied to their ignorance of the Bible, and could be the reason they were targeted.

Aliens appear fearless and in firm control when dealing with humans. However, in one case there was evidence of aliens exhibiting fear of a human female. She was abducted and struggled against the alien creatures as they tried to do something to her leg (she felt pain). The aliens were unhappy with her lack of cooperation. She indicated they took

blood from her leg. They told her that no one will
believe her (story). She said, "Yes, they will, I'll find
a priest, I'll find a church." After she utters her threat,
she finds herself almost instantly back in her bed.[4]
Could the mere hint to invoke a legitimate spiritual
authority stop the intrusion? It certainly seems possible. Perhaps they fear the ultimate authority, when
one calls on God.

The Bible warns us, "...*the enemy goes about like a roar-
ing lion seeking whom he may devour...*" (1 Peter 5:8). Without Jesus we are vulnerable. There is a constant
need to be alert and spiritually in tune with God if we
are going to resist being cannon fodder for Satan.
Above all we need to realize that the protective covering of the *Blood of Jesus* is more than a match against
any of Satan's disguises or devices.

A persistent observation kept surfacing during
my research. I found no instance where a victim had
rebuked the aliens in the name of Jesus. Maybe they
didn't know they could. However, it would have been
interesting to know what would have happened, had
they done it. A nagging concern for some is; "What
can be done, for a person who goes through the
Luciferic Initiation and buys into the New Age doctrines?" In other words, once a person becomes an
initiate of Lucifer can they be set free? The answer
to this question is a definite YES!!

Deliverance although, is not easy since the individual embraced the initiation by their actions and
thought patterns. Spiritual blindness that results from
demonic wisdom makes it difficult for a person to
see or admit their error. (a definite requirement for
repentance)

Prayer is the key to breaking Satan's hold on a person. God is THE master in setting up circumstances to expose the falsehood New Agers have embraced. It may take persistent prayer over a period of time to see the results. Prayer will dispense God's grace to the person, who can then be made aware of their error and repent. In order for the Luciferic Initiation to be effective, it is necessary to trick a person, or people group, into believing they are doing good, (or are "born good") and are on the right track. The trappings are usually wrapped in a very human, warm and caring New Age attitude. Again— *Sincere effective prayer* is the most effective way to break Satan's hold in the battle for the human soul.

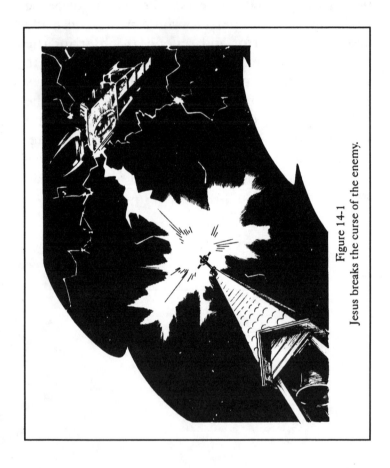

Figure 14-1
Jesus breaks the curse of the enemy.

15
What About the Children?

Children are extremely at risk from the invasion of alien and demonic forces. Fantasy video games, gruesome cartoons, ouija boards, and mind games like Dungeons and Dragons are the lures that will attract the young mind. Children are very susceptible (and gullible). They are easy targets for training and indoctrination.

Parents have an enormous task in helping children to filter out and reject things potentially harmful to them. Not all cartoons or video games are dangerous. However tremendous opportunity for the wrong things to be viewed exists due to high parental acceptance and easy access into homes through television. We have been conditioned by de-sensitization to accept the almost continuous viewing of violence and casual immorality.

Many parents assume that the entertainment industry will look after their moral interests and what is being fed to their children. Nothing is further from the truth. Responsibility for the home and the child, belong to whoever is in charge there. Even Congress who seems concerned for the child, in their own ineffectual way, tries to curb the video's impact on the young mind. Children are not mature enough to make decisions. Parents and guardians must be held accountable to God for what they allow—He will not listen to contrary liberal explanations.

How far can children go before getting into trouble with demonic or alien forces? The magnitude of this question is very far reaching in scope. A Christian friend told me of an incident where one of their children saw and talked to a fantasy person who came and visited with the child. This event raised serious concerns in the parent about how this could happen. Another chilling incident was covered in *"Communion."* A mother wrote to the author about her two-year old child who recognized the alien face on the cover of his book and said, "He's bad." Apparently the man (the alien) took his toys and never gave them back. The mother goes on to mention that there were many missing toys from their house.

Children affected by strange experiences are unable to explain the circumstances. Parents usually ignore or overlook children's stories, chalking it up to being a product of their imaginations...until the problem is clearly manifest. It is only when the problem is obvious do the parents or guardians begin to look for answers.

A very good book on the subject of Children's vulnerability is entitled, *"Like Lambs to the Slaughter"* by Johanna Michelson . Another book highly recommended on the subject is *"Children at Risk"* by author Dr. James C. Dobson. These are troubled and treacherous times for anyone raising a family today.

School Agendas

My wife related an observation that her father made back in the 1950's when she was a small girl attending school. He felt teachers were conveying the attitude to students that their parents were really quite stupid. In the 1950's, however, school was a relatively uncomplicated affair and parents still held primary control over their offspring. Today, I wonder if her father may have been prophetic and ahead of his time, by the looks of this day and age!

Children spend a large percentage of their time within the public school system. This fact should raise questions concerning indoctrination. The New Age philosophy now appearing in our schools has stripped the educational system of standard traditional values. They now teach many secular subjects like *situational ethics, *values clarification, and alternative lifestyles while freely giving advice and information concerning abortion to minors, with no thought of the parents who are legally responsible for that minor. These issues have long lasting affects on our society and our children, undermining their parent's authority and chosen value system. Ultimately, the children's attitude will also affect society as well.

What seems to be emerging is a plan by schools to undermine parental control. The state is slowley assuming the complete teaching function. Students are introduced to alternative standards and lifestyles to choose from, where moral ethics can be whatever they want them to be.

Under the banner of education, all hell (and its agenda) is breaking loose on the kids! We are paying dearly by this assault on the family unit and the damage done to our children as a result. The answer from many school administrators and teacher unions seem to be the same...more money to solve the problem with. Money has never been the answer by itself and never will be, but the quest for it continues.

Some years ago my wife and I discovered the failure of the boondoggle," known as the "open" classroom being implemented in the California schools. As a teacher's aide, my wife personally observed the "classroom turned free-for-all," with noise levels high enough to stress out even the toughest little campers.

Happily, she was assigned to a teacher who maintained an "old fashioned and orderly" room for her students. To the dismay of the liberals, who had touted the wonders of the "open" classroom, this teacher's students always maintained higher levels of academic achievement than those assigned to the madhouses that were "open." I hope this idea was abandoned, but I am not positive as we moved out of state. Again, someone thought "change" had to be good. It's time we stopped experimenting with our children and started implementing programs that have been time tested and proven effective. Must every generation be a guinea pig for the laboratories of the liberal?

Maybe it is time Christian parents looked into the so-called credentials of educators, and of the Masters and Ph.D degrees that have been handed out. Let's question the motives of these people who want to change society through our children. Just what is their agenda and what do they believe? Diplomas, no matter how they highly they are esteemed, rarely tell much about the person's character or personal biases.

One home school parent made a search into the Washington State sponsored school "reform" programs under the label of *America 2000*. What she found was startling. The roots of this program go back to the teachings and influence of Alice Bailey and her channel spirit. She was a well known New Age guru and cultist of her time. Is this what the fight is all about?

It's time for the American public to demand proper standards for those who teach our children and are paid with our tax dollars. Nothing else will do. Reform programs would not be needed if the schools were doing what they are paid to do...and that is to teach basic education. When it comes to teaching New Age ideas and moral aspects of life in school, we should insist on knowing the basis of any disseminated information. If parental guidance is ignored or refused, we have three options:

1) remove the kids and place them in private schools.
2) replace school officials with those that respond to parental interests.
3) utilize home schooling—a practice rapidly gaining popularity in this country.

Parents must regain control of their children's education. No institution should ever have the mandate to supersede family authority and it's values.

16

New Age Religion

Aliens don't reveal much about their feelings on religion. As mentioned in chapter eleven, they acknowledge a supreme being or universal light. One that sustains all life. The subject of religion is avoided, except in rare instances. I believe the lack of any religious acknowledgment is part of Satan's plan to provoke people into questioning the role of God in the universe. This could be the reason why alternative belief systems and ideals are constantly proposed. It may be why we are being prepared for some awesome galactic spiritual wonder... which is about to be sprung upon us.

In the book of Revelation, one-third of the heavenly host are to be cast out of God's presence. Could Satan, and his disgraced ones, comprise that part of heaven still under siege? (I may add that this is not the heaven where the throne of God is).

Until Satan falls to earth, we might be dealing with a blend of heavenly host operating in the universe (referred to in the Bible as the *heavenlies). The blend is probably made up of both good and bad host, similar to humankind here on earth. This deduction should not be surprising since it is Biblically supported. The heavens contain both good and bad spirit beings (angels). Up until now, my "gut feeling" has been that all aliens were demonic in nature.

The Bible identifies angelic host as messengers from God. Aliens never clearly identify themselves as being God's messengers. They keep their identity as nebulous as possible, and this is an important point for the saints of God to remember.

Proof of God identifying his messengers can be found in the Biblical account of Daniel. Daniel's Prayer was answered immediately by God. However, the angel bringing the answer was held back by the "Prince of Greece" for twenty-one days.[1] This obviously was not a human prince—but a powerful evil spiritual prince (host) operating in a *heavenly realm*. The angel from God, identified itself as Gabriel, and delivered the message.

Billy Graham appeared on a PBS television program with talk show host, David Frost, Sunday, January 31, 1993.[2] As expected, Frost asked Mr. Graham many questions pertaining to religion. During a discussion of heaven and the universe, Billy stated that he believes there is life on other planets. He further speculated that we may one day have the job of bringing the gospel salvation message to other planets.

I don't know if life exists on other planets. However, this conversation with Graham does bring into perspective a possible future relationship with a heavenly host. If they *are* from God, being a part of His plan, all well and good. However, if they are not...we must be ready as Christians to deal with them according to the Holy Bible.

Meanwhile, I hold steadfastly to the facts in the Bible, as they are unchangeable. Safety is with Jesus, and not in the so-called aliens—whom we don't know. Mankind does not need any more confusion or deception than we already experience as it is. The author of "*The Watchers*," mentions that alien information given to the abductee, Betty Andreasson, will revolutionize every aspect of our lives. Whatever we now know of science, religion, philosophy, and sociology will be seriously changed![3] God has revealed no such plan, except for the dire warnings spoken about in chapter 24 of Matthew. Here He speaks of many false prophets who arise and mislead many.[4] Not all false prophets will come to us looking and sounding like Jesus: Who really knows what they will look like.

In her awe inspiring encounter, Betty Andreasson was taken to meet the "One." The experience was so fantastic, filled with such dazzling colors that she couldn't describe the beauty and power of what she saw. For this event she was taken to an underground base by an alien and passed mysteriously through a huge glass door.[5] I can only imagine who the "One" is, but I feel certain it is not God.

The only place under the earth that the Bible refers to, is Hell. What did she really see? Was it Satan disguised as an angel of light? Through these overpowering events, Christians can begin to detect how strategically people are being prepared for adventures that will result in confusing their traditional belief in God.

A New Religion in the Making

The *Out of Body Experience* (OBE) and *Near Death Experience* (NDE) events are "happening to just about everybody"—that is if you believe the rash of books on the subject. I believe most OBE and NDE are false and misleading experiences preparing man for a new religion, (all part of the Luciferic Initiation).

The experiences are clever and sound good. Christians and non-Christians alike are becoming enamored with this new revelation of what heaven will be like. The reason it sounds so good is because these experiences come from a broad spectrum of reasonable and hurting people. Many went through a wonderful life changing event under a life threatening situation. The flood of books on the subject are from doctors, and nurses, as well as average folk who underwent these experiences.

While a few have shown Godly discernment about OBE/NDE, (like Maurice S. Rawlings, M.D. in *"To Hell and Back,"*) most seem to mix traditional religious beliefs with ideas that don't fit with the Bible. For example: In one NDE case, a woman says she was taken to a place on another planet where the people were very kind, but busy. Some were gardening and some were involved in elaborate building construction. The place was very beautiful and had lots of lush green plants. The natives were all very loving and caring. They appeared to be very similar to us, except happier. This certainly sounds wonderful and enticing but, for us on earth, this is not supported by the Bible. These events describe a very happy place, i.e., one that sounds so good that it might lead people to believe God kept something back. They may believe that He is just now revealing it to us.

God has not described heaven as some distant planet, like some religions and cults have done. People involved in building construction on another planet is not covered anywhere in the Bible as a future job description. Children present on that planet is another

clue that something is wrong. Jesus said, "In heaven
they neither marry or are given in marriage."[6] Where
did the children come from? In addition, God also said,
"No eye has seen nor ear has heard all that God has prepared...for
those who love Him."[7]

Is God changing His word to us now? Is He revealing things previously hidden? I think not! If this were
so, then we could not trust any of His word. God would
be like us, unstable, and erratic. It's that simple.

Medical scientists are also entering the OBE and
NDE arena by studying the brain and trying to understand these events. Some have already gone out on a
limb through the use of special electronic devices, (that
induce certain brain stimuli) suggesting that the events
are caused by low blood circulation in the brain. Please
take note of the confusion from experts trying to explain this phenomenon.

A world of hurting people battered and bruised from
the assaults of evil agendas, broken hearts and unkind
people (including churches) are ready to accept and
embrace another way to heaven.

The Church of Jesus Christ has often failed to bring
the healing balm of God who told us how to receive it.
Instead, churches now turn to secular remedies for ad-
dictions, abuse, alternative life styles, and so forth. In
some cases, the church still takes a stand against a particular evil like abortion. However, the stand is hardly
mentioned from the pulpit anymore. If it is, it is ane-
mic at best. Has the all-encompassing "New Age" inner light and peace at any cost principle...made it taboo
to disturb people about sin and hell anymore? Is the
church of Jesus Christ ready to tackle the issue of OBE,
as well as explain what it's all about? Are we ready and
able to do that?

Universal Citizens

An abductee, interviewed on a popular late night radio talk show program, revealed some interesting philosophical information about how the aliens see us. The individual said that aliens refer to the earth as a plane of separation. Earthlings are invited to join (the rest of) the universe through love, as "universal citizens."

It was also mentioned that humans confuse individuality with independence and are to learn to be responsible for the harmony of the whole. Even though everyone is invited, aliens realize that not everyone will accept the invitation. Some earthlings are more advanced in esoteric ability than others. When asked if anyone can make themselves available to the abduction experience, the person said, aliens look for a matching vibration (*resonating field frequencies) before they make a selection for a visitation.

In my mind, this "matching vibration" represents the mechanism of how a person is selected. As mentioned previously, energy vibrations are the key to who is selected. The vibration signal a person sends is the determining factor for an alien connection.

He went on to say that aliens are working to create a critical mass (explosion) of their spirituality. The abductee claimed to have been implanted with some type of bio-implant, which fine tunes the brain with enhanced spiritual capability.

When asked about God, there was only a vague explanation from this abductee. He mentions these aliens are not gods, but guardians or caretakers of planet earth. They explain God away as the "greater thing," and we are to seek Him as the idea of unity.

New Agers and abductees who believe these explanations are in serious trouble. They have given themselves over to another ideology. Although some aliens
sound kind and loving, their message needs to be dis-
sected to find the real meaning. It appears another kind
of love is involve...A humanistic love, not a Godly love.

As researcher Bud Hopkins has pointed out from
his work, aliens seem to be modifying abductees for
some higher purpose they have in mind. Why the modification? Did God make a mistake with his creation and
now has sent in spiritual mechanics for the fix? As for
their comment about working with humans to create a
critical mass, that's probably true. They are working
toward ways to get as many humans as possible into
their camp in order to force a spiritual change in the
course of human destiny.

Critical mass is a good term. It implies the enemy is
building an army. When they modify enough people,
creating followers, they will have sufficient power from
the swollen ranks of their believers to implement a spiritual change on earth. This growth pattern will probably
continue to increase for some time yet. To detect the
results of this evil explosion we must look for the whole-
sale attitude changes in man, and in society as time goes
on. It is very oblivious that a *paradigm shift will occur
in a widespread fashion. We Christians must be on the
alert to see it when it happens.

What is the Alien Motive?

Aliens performing beneficent surgery and providing cures for diseases seem noble. However, their real
motive for providing these cures is not known. From
alien comments, patterns begin to emerge within their

proclaimed intent of assisting mankind. These patterns reveal specific information that might suggest their overall motive. They are as follows:

1. They claim to be "caretakers of form" on earth. (Allegedly they have taken the seed of man, and all living things to "protect" them from destructive forces on earth. Sound like an intergalactic environmental protection agency?)

2. They acknowledge a universal light force in the universe and this light force sustains all life.

3. Abductees are taken to meet the "One" in the interior of the earth. Who lives in the bowels of the earth?

4. Most visits occur during the night time hours. Is this because human beings are easier to access and open to receive spiritual invasion at night?

5. In one case, an alien admitted to creating illusions. This statement alone is enough to put the whole alien masquerade in serious question.

6. Aliens have another perspective of time and space. (The past, present and future is NOW for them). Can only spiritual creatures exist in a timeless mode?

7. They are preparing to evolve man's society, science, religion, philosophy, etc..

8. Most alien ideas conform to New Age ideals.
   a. Channeling
   b. Out of Body Experiences and Near Death Experiences
   c. No recognition of Jesus
   d. A god of universal light
   e. Earth is a living entity
   f. Humanistic caring

g. Reincarnation—other lives
h. Shamanism

Aliens have shown an interest to train mankind in a new spiritual science. This certainly is a strong possibility...especially when one considers how much occult material is being warmly embraced by the general public. New Age writers believe they can weave our lives together with technical advances of the alien world. They set themselves up to be exploited under the assumptions that:

1) aliens would bother to share their technology with us and we suffer no consequences, and...
2) these foreign beings are benevolent and trustworthy.

If aliens can influence and control human beings, through mind control methods, then perhaps they can spiritually inhabit abductees to carry out the Luciferic Plan on Earth. It is fairly obvious their plan seems to rationally use evil powers embodied in the human frame to mingle with society, gaining positions of authority and stature. By doing this, they become the wolves in sheep's clothing, (in this case human bodies) preparing to take control of the world. Some writers have suggested that human abductees are modified and programmed for future use. These modified humans would spring to action, on some sort of a signal or command. What a chilling thought. Could this already be happening? Is the fruit of the *New World Order* evident already? By all accounts in the daily news, I think we may be there now.

As stated previously, Man's intellect and wrongful pursuit of knowledge (adventure into the unknown) is the culprit for man's trip into the New Age dilemma. I think it was Karl Marx who said religion is the opiate of the masses: I contend that currently the opiate of the masses is our insatiable hunger and thirst for knowledge. What mankind needs is the wisdom and discernment God gives to handle knowledge. Man's intellect and knowledge can only build up pride. When abused, man's intellect and knowledge are a great team that is a prime target for the enemy to use against him. Lucifer manipulates them both to raise a person up for the fall.

William Cooper, the author of *"Behold a Pale Horse,"* said it well when he stated: *"The worship (a lot different from study) of knowledge, science, or technology is Satanism in its purest form, and it's god is Lucifer."*[8] He mentions that the power base of secret societies is usually found through the use of specific knowledge and mysteries. He believes this all springs from Lucifer in the garden when Adam and Eve were enticed to eat of the tree of knowledge—which "freed" man from the bonds of ignorance, and enslaved him to sin.

The clues mentioned above together with many others not mentioned seem to point to serious questions about alien motives. Too much of their effort is wrapped up in secrecy and mind control, therefore making them difficult to reveal. However, from the many bits and pieces of inconsistent alien statements, we can perceive a unholy plan at work against man.

Heavenly Host

The term, "heavenly host" needs to be discussed from a Biblical standpoint. I have always thought the term, "heavenly host" was another name for angels or God's army. I have discovered this is not always the case. The Biblical term, "heavenly host" includes more than just angels, (or God's army). It is the greater category term, including all of God's created beings, except man, (but possibly him also). God's created beings are identified in the Bible as follows:

1. Angels, seraphim, cherubim, archangels, powers, and principalities.
2. Four living creatures.
3. Twenty-four elders.
4. Sons of God.
5. Lucifer/Satan
6. Fallen angels, demons, princes, evil spirits, and chained demons.

Figure 16-1 is a simple, graphic depiction of the heavenly host and how they might fit into Biblical meaning. The Bible does not say God made evil ones. He made them all perfect with free will. They choose to rebel and now represent the fallen host.

If aliens have the ability to control their coming and going at will...in a space time continuum, they simply have to be spiritual creations. If they are the fallen rebellious ones flying around in the heavens, they have a surprise coming to them. The prophet Isaiah [24:1-22] indicates, the host of heaven will be punished during the end time when the earth goes through great upheaval and earthquakes. I believe this will be a time when all of the evil powers on high will be finally dealt with and put under punishment. That includes all the various faces of the enemy in terms of aliens, angels of light, false religious apparitions, and powerful, evil beings, (as seen down through the ages) that operate in the heavenlies.

A New Road to Nirvana

"*Virtual Reality" is going to become the modern high-tech road to Nirvana. The wonders of Virtual Reality will become mind teasing and addictive. Preliminary use of this computer simulation concept is already a popular hit in game arcades and training programs. Virtual Reality is still in its infancy. It has not yet been sufficiently developed into what it will become for society in the future. The refining process for this product will eventually become a trillion dollar enterprise, when it is coupled with interactive television.

There are features of Virtual Reality that will put mankind securely into an imaginary world without the use of drugs. This world will prove to be a poisonous, yet mind bending challenge for us all here on earth.

Russ Wagner, a Virtual Reality specialist, made some interesting but ominous comments on the Art Bell, late night Radio program on September 13, 1994. He indicated people who undergo the Virtual Reality experience enter a state similar to a person under the influence of drugs. He suggests that when a person goes into deeper and deeper "virtual concentration", they enter a trance state of mind similar to hypnosis. I can see where a trance could hold a person in a quasi-prison of their own making, or of someone else's fabricated fantasy.

A person could choose to live in a virtual world, if it provided stimulation and experiences (thrills) more desirable than the real world they live in. For example:

Paralyzed people might prefer life in a "virtual world" if it mentally liberates them from the confines of their body, and provides a feeling of accomplishing feats. They might be able to climb up a dangerous, but challenging mountain, or swim in a virtual pool under beautiful conditions, or fly a fighter airplane with fancy maneuvers. Through their minds, they could attain control over their limited physical world. Is this not what everyone wants in life? To be free of their limitations...no matter what they may be? This is what religions of every kind promise in the afterlife. Some go as far as to promise freedom from limitations in this life as well.

The *Virtual Reality trance will train a person to live in a quasi-spiritual state. It will open the mind to altered states of consciousness. Virtual Reality will be a new, but more effective way to become an initiate of Lucifer. It is a way to come under Satan's control while still maintaining a look of respectability. All the flower children of the 60's had to do is take a trip to Nirvana was Pot, LSD and a VW bus. That era had a lasting impact on society. Now society gets to enter a sophisticated high- tech electronic trip to Nirvana through Virtual Reality.

A scary look at where we might be heading was covered briefly by a story found in the 16th anniversary (1994) issue of Omni Magazine. The story tells of a person who became a computer network junkie. He tried desperately to quit the Internet—timers, automatic disconnects, everything—but he was hooked to a mind teaser. Virtual Reality, has the frightening potential of becoming much more addictive than what this person experienced on a simple computer network. Russ Wagner said people might have to receive a reality check every fifteen minutes or so, just to make sure they don't enter into this "lala land of hypnosis"...a very scary possibility.

Here are some examples of "Virtual Reality satisfactions":

1. FOOTBALL
Virtual Reality, will plug an arm chair football enthusiast right into the virtual game. A person can run touchdowns, kick field goals and get in the opponents face. With all the sights, sounds and grunts included. Yes, even to the point of smelling the sweat and feeling the pounding. Carefully, of course.

2. THEATER
Become part of a virtual theater production by participating with Virtual actors and dialog. It will also be possible to sit in the theater and witness a past historical event, at least someone's interpretation of it.

3. SPACE TRAVEL
Just imagine! You can travel through inter-solar and inter-galactic space with space ships, UFOs, etc. Become part of the adventure of discovering new worlds and beings. Participate in life-like space battles, start and create new worlds, just like on Startrek!

4. VIRTUAL CHURCH
Would it not be just divine to attend the First Church of Virtual Reality? A place where everyone puts on a special apparatus that would focus laser images onto the retina of a person's eye. Programs that produce images of Jesus and the Apostle Paul will allow you to see and communicate with them. How wonderful it will be to experience early Christianity. Sounds

exciting, doesn't it? However, it is just another deception to open up our minds to more *Lying Wonders* of our age. Could this be the image of the Beast? Not a beast like an animal. Rather a beast of invention, automation and mechanism. An image that always changes shape and form, and yet provides challenge and adventure. This would not be an unchanging image like an ancient idol or statue. Surely this can't be what we were warned about...is it?

5. THE ULTIMATE GOAL

To encourage a person to enter into a place of such ecstasy, that he or she would lose all desire to eat or drink. Remaining in such a state for a prolonged periods of time will cause a person's mind to merge with the virtual program and become an integral part of the illusion. By strengthening the focus of the trance into pure concentration a person could opt to leave their earth given reality permanently. This person might complete the transition into a new altered reality. In other words, he or she is lulled into a form of suicide by the power of his or her own will! Result...Nirvana to virtual interpretation...to mental illness, and/or death. In any case, "Welcome to Hell!"—the ultimate deception.

Satan will always be up to his same old tricks until the Lord throws him into his eternal Lake of Fire.

Reality

Many of us refer to reality in every day life as if we know what it is. But what is the standard for it? Is there a standard? Do governmental and private agencies have their own standard? Does society have a standard for reality? These questions are crucial.

Psychology and Psychiatry have defined reality—but what is their standard based on? I presume to tackle this issue because it becomes very important in light of what may be happening to humanity through these alien forces. In trying to grapple with the concepts of this subject, I had to develop an overall understanding that branched out into three main categories: (1)"Our Reality," (2)"Other Realities," and (3)"God's Reality." These three are all quite different from each other and play an important role in understanding the end time deceptions.

Our Reality

The reality we live in was created by God. We are familiar with "our" reality because it is the one we grew up with. Most of us can relate to the world we live in and to the surroundings common to this environment. In other words, we can all agree what we consider real and normal to us, in general. Consequently, we can also do the same for those things not real to us. In that sense, there are limits (or boundaries) we are willing to accept, defining our reality. This is exactly what most of us do to control our sphere of existence in this world. God created this world and put us in it to fulfill the gift of life. He obviously has a reason for doing this. In addition, He gave us the rules for life here on earth. These rules are found in the Bible.

The Bible, its associated history, prophecies, revelations, stories, and personal events were given to us by the Holy Spirit for the express purpose of revealing God's restoration plan for a fallen, sinful human race. This created reality on earth, although is temporal. According to the prophets, the Gospels and other Biblical accounts, this reality will end. Meanwhile, we must protect against anything that introduces another reality, one which modifies, or promotes a "better" reality other than the one God gave us. All other realities fabricated or modified, must be viewed with suspicion, especially if it introduces new teachings and revelations contrary to the Bible.

Other Realities

Dream Reality

Most of us have encountered a dream state which is not the one we live in. Dream states can range from normal real life experiences, to supernatural, bizarre and unrealistic experiences, both in it's content and plot. Some dreams have realistic meaning, but they are usually dismissed because they can not be easily interpreted or understood. Not all dreams contain coded messages.

Extreme Realities

An example of an extreme reality might be someone with mental and emotional psychological disturbances which cloud or confuse their perception of the average, or normal societal behavior. Extreme realities can result from mental, physical, biological or chemical inducements. In addition, they can also be induced by a variety of demonic influences.

Fabricated Realities

Virtual reality, video games, movies, games or books of fantasy are fabricated realities that some people like to spend a lot of time on. They are fabricated because someone had to create them. Fabricated realities, taken to the furthest degree will lead a person into ungodly spiritual experiences. Most people cannot discern when they have gone too far, taking these fabricated realities to the furthest degree...unknowingly. It is better not to play with fire at all.

Spiritual Realities

Spiritual realities (other than God's Reality) include such things as the occult, witchcraft, Satanic practices, New Age concepts and practices, Extra Sensory Perception (ESP), astral travel and other para-normal activities. These spiritual realities are all in direct opposition to God's reality. They are essentially alternative spiritual realities, being induced by demonic, supernatural power.

Another Reality

A reality that exists outside, or in addition to the one our society lives in. *Example:* UFO/alien existence (a different space and time dimension or continuum and communities on other planet systems). There seems to be ample evidence that God has created these other realities.

Relative Realities

This is inclusive of clubs, lodges, secret societies, fraternal, institutional or work environment. In our normal everyday life, we usually associate with some type of group or function which has a definite impact on us. These relative realities (or experiences) give us the opportunity to develop and absorb ideals and thoughts from others who help make up our identities. This can be a good or bad experience, depending on what we embrace and accept in the process. There are many relative realities that affect us as we grow and develop.

I'm certainly not the last word on the subject of reality. My attempt is to simply suggest that other realities have a significant impact on a person's life. UFOs and aliens, for example, represent another reality that could be the greatest shock and deception man will ever have to face in this life. Other Realities, or envelopes of existence, can disturb our God-given existence. They can actually replace our God-given reality with a completely different set of life values—in total opposition to what was originally intended for us.

God's Reality

My quest for truth led me through a lot of strange and unusual material. I began to ask myself serious questions about what is real, and what is fiction. Making sense of reality became very difficult while reviewing UFO/alien encounters. However, I kept my feet on The Solid Rock, Jesus Christ while going through it. He is the ultimate reality.

Each time I tried to deal with alien events from my reality perspective, I found they were not what I thought they were. In fact, I tried to make sense out of the data researched bringing me to the ultimate question: *What is the definition of reality?*

The American Heritage Dictionary of the English Language (New College Edition) defines reality as:

1. The quality or state of being actual or true. 2. A person, entity, or event that is actual. 3. The totality of all things possessing actuality, existence, or essence. 4. That which exists objec-

tively and in fact. 5. The sum of all that is real, absolute, and unchangeable.

I am so glad that my God is an unchangeable God. ("Jesus Christ is the same yesterday and today, yes and forever." Hebrews 13:8). That is my REALITY!

At the appropriate time, God will end our created environment that we are so familiar with—and He will introduce us to: His ACTUALITY, i.e. That which is finally real! This will be the greatest and most wonderful event in our existence for those who believe and confess His name. At the same time, it will be the most terrifying for those who have ignored Him.

He is the only true reality, although His reality is visually veiled from us while we live on earth. The glimpse of His reality is what is revealed in His Word. The Bible has many passages concerning heaven and the afterlife, but very few descriptions of it. God's reality is initiated for those who accept Him on earth in their hearts.

God's Reality is eternal, while ours is an *interim temporal envelope, a place where we are put to a test to see if we will simply be obedient to His commandments...(rules). He regards loyalty and obedience, more precious than anything we can think of, and no one enters His Reality without passing the test of life, namely belief in his son Jesus Christ of Nazareth. All other beliefs lead to death. Those who fail this test here on earth will not receive a second chance. They cannot re-cycle themselves...(no reincarnation), and they won't evolve into some higher life form if their "karma" is good. Instead, they will be given over to their delusions and lusts while they live. They will be allowed to indulge themselves to the fullest (including other beliefs and New Age ideals) before experiencing the Final Reality...judgment for all eternity.

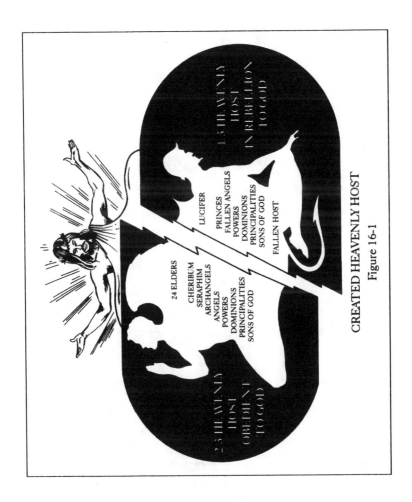

2/3 HEAVENLY HOST OBEDIENT TO GOD

24 ELDERS
CHERIBUM
SERAPHIM
ARCHANGELS
ANGELS
POWERS
DOMINIONS
PRINCIPALITIES
SONS OF GOD

1/3 HEAVENLY HOST IN REBELLION TO GOD

LUCIFER

PRINCES
FALLEN ANGELS
POWERS
DOMINIONS
PRINCIPALITIES
SONS OF GOD

FALLEN HOST

CREATED HEAVENLY HOST

Figure 16-1

About the Author

Robert R. Kaminski is a retired Boeing Aerospace engineering executive. He received a Bachelor of Science degree in Electrical Engineering Communications from The Milwaukee School of Engineering. Mr. Kaminski has been engaged in the Christian charismatic renewal for the past fifteen years, and is currently involved in various Christian denominational and non-denominational outreaches.

His interest in UFO's began in 1953, while he was on active duty in the U.S. Navy. While on training exercises in the Gulf of Mexico, he observed a strange plot on a radar screen aboard the USS Monterey (CVL-26).

For many years prior to this, the author dismissed UFO's as a figment of other people's imagination. His skepticism came primarily because of questionable stories (published and unpublished). Although most importantly UFO phenomenon was not an issue clearly covered in the Bible. He needed to get some answers.

After becoming a student of the Bible, the author began to look for the answer. This commenced his research and posed the question, "If flying saucers were not specifically covered in the Bible, then how do we account for these strange reports from reasonable people?"

"Lying Wonders: Evil Encounter of a Close Kind," is a work comprised of the fall-out research discovered while determining the spiritual aspect of UFO's.

Notes

Chapter One

1. Bosveld, Jane: (1994, October) Cathedral Dreams. Omni. p.8.
2. Alnor, William M.: UFOs in the NEW AGE: Baker Book House, Grand Rapids 1992, pp. 146
3. Ibid., pp. 146.
4. Ibid., pp. 146.
5. Marrs, Texe: Mystery Mark of the New Age: Crossway Books, Westchester 1988, pp. 234-235.
6. Ibid., pp. 235.
7. Marrs, Texe: quotes on Benjamin Creme: Mystery Mark of the New Age: Crossway Books, Westchester 1988, pp. 235.

Chapter Two

1. NASB Proverbs 14:12
2. NASB Ecclesiastes 1:9
3. Rawlings, Maurice S. M.D.: To Hell and Back: Thomas Nelson Publishers: Nashville 1993, pp.160

Chapter Three

1. "Playing God" at the National Institutes of Health, Our Sunday Visitor 30 Oct., 1994.

Chapter Four

1. Voice Network International: Over My Dead Body: Arlington Heights 1989.

Chapter Five

1. Good, Timothy: The UFO Report: Avon Books, New York 1989, pp. 224.
2. Ibid., pp. 89-91.

Chapter Six

1. Briggs, David. "Genesis Word Pattern Suggest Divine Writing." Tacoma News Tribuine 29 October 1995:
2. Kelly, Chiristina. "Port Angeles Witch defies image, see herself as healer and helper." Tacoma News Tribune 28 Aug. 1995:
3. Braden, Greg: Awakening to Zero Point: Sacred Spaces: Ann Arbor 1994, pp. 70.

Chapter Seven

1. Spangler, David/Thomson, William Irwin: Reimagination of the World, Bear and Co. Inc.: Santa Fe 1991, pp. 148.

2. Strieber, Whitley: Transformation: Avon Books, New York 1988, pp. 48

3. Strieber, Whitley: Communion: Avon Books, New York 1987, pp. Inside cover page.

4. Ibid., pp. 47-48.

5. Ibid., pp. 19.

6. Ibid., pp. 76-77.

7. Strieber, Whitley: Transformation: Avon Books, New York, 1988, pp. 67.

8. Ibid., pp. 47.

9. Strieber, Whitley: Communion: Avon Books, New York 1987, pp. 76, 102.

10. Strieber, Whitley: Transformation: Avon Books, New York 1988, pp. 30.

11. Ibid., pp. 27-30.

12. Ibid., pp. 209.

13. Ibid., pp. 73.

14. Ibid., pp. 36.

15. Ibid., pp. 79.

16. Ibid., pp. 79.

17. Ibid., pp. 79.

18. Ibid., pp. 79.

19. Ibid., pp. 109.

20. Strieber, Whitley: Transformation: Avon Books, Neww York 1988, pp. 110.

21. Ibid., pp. 190-191.

22. NASB Heb. 12:2.

23. Strieber, Whitley: Transformation: Avon Books, New York 1988, pp. 196.

24. Ibid., pp. 209.
25. Fowler, Raymond E.: The Watchers: Bantam Books, New York 1991, pp. 149.
26. Ibid., pp. 150.
27. Ibid., pp. 152.
28. Strieber, Whitley: Transformation: Avon Books, New York 1988, pp. 209.
29. Ibid., pp. 242.
30. Ibid., pp. 242.
31. Ibid., pp. 251.
32. Ibid., pp. 252.
33. NASB, Jas. 4:7.
34. Strieber, Whitley: Transformation: Avon Books, New York 1988, pp. 256.
35. Ibid., pp. 256.
36. Ibid., pp. 256.
37. Ibid., pp. 257.
38. Ibid., pp. 258.
39. Strieber, Whitley: Transformation: Avon Books, New York 1988, pp. 258.
40. Strieber, Whitley: Transformation: Avon Books, New York 1988, pp. 258.

Chapter Nine

1. DK DIRECT LIMITED: UFO: The Continuing Enigma, Readers Digest, New York 1991, pp. 118.
2. Steiger, Brad and Sherry Hansen: The Rainbow Conspiracy: Pinnacle Books-Windsor Publishing Corp, New York 1994, pp. 160.
3. Good, Timothy : Above Top Secret: Quill William Morrow, New York 1988, pp. 118.

4. Cooper, William: Behold a Pale Horse: Light Technology Publishing, Sedona Arizona 1991, pp. 200.
5. Ibid., pp. 200.
6. Ibid., pp. 200.
7. Ibid., pp. 202-213.

Chapter Ten

1. Fiore, Edith: Encounters: Ballantine Books, New York 1989. pp. 153.
2. Ibid., pp. 166-167.
3. Ibid., pp. 157.
4. Ibid., pp. 158.
5. Fiore, Edith: Encounters: Ballantine Books, New York 1989, pp. 157-158.
6. Ibid., pp. 157.
7. Roberts, C.R. "Mount Ranier-Area youth has close encounter in the foothills." Tacoma News Tribune 24 April 1994.

Chapter Eleven

1. Fiore, Edith: Encounters: Ballantine Books, New York 1989 pp. 249.
2. Ibid., pp. 226.
3. Ibid., pp. 85.
4. Ibid., pp. 85.
5. Ibid., pp. 85.

Chapter Twelve

1. "The Alien Abduction Syndrome," After Dark Newsletter (Dreamland Report) Oct. 1995.
2. "Vatican Telescope" Tacoma News Tribune Dec. 19, (A-1) 1992 Reprinted from Arizona Republic.
3. Freedenthal, Stacy. "Calling UFOs: Parking available, no waiting." Tacoma News Tribune 26 Dec. 1992 reprinted from Dallas Morning News.
4. "UfO Mysteries Solved in Bible." Sun 17 May, 1994:
5. Alexander, Ben: Out From Darkness: College Publishing Co. Joplin, 1985 pp. 36.
6. Ibid., pp. 36.
7. Alexander, Ben: Out From Darkness: College Publishing Co. Joplin, 1985 pp. 36.
8. Fowler, Raymond E.: The Watchers: Bantam Books, New York 1990 pp. 237.
9. Lindemann, Michael: UfOs and the Alien Presence Six Viewpoints: 2020 Group, Santa Barbara 1991 pp. 80-81.
10. Fowler, Raymond E.: The Watchers: Bantam Books, New York 1990 pp. 204.

Chapter Thirteen

1. Strieber, Whitley: Transformation: Avon Books, New York, 1988. pp. 93.
2. Fiore, Edith: Encounters: Ballantine Books, New York, 1989. pp. 123.
3. Strieber, Whitley: Communion: Avon Books, New York, 1987. pp. 237.
4. Ibid., pp. 300.

Chapter Fourteen

1. Fowler, Raymond: The Watchers: Bantam Books, New York, 1990, pp. 184.
2. Steiger, Brad, and Sherry Hansen: The Rainbow Conspiricy: Pinnacle Books-Windsor Publishing Corp. New York 1994. pp. 9.
3. Strieber, Witley: Transformation: Avon Books: New York, 1987 pp. 36.
4. Fiore, Edith: Encounters: Ballantine Books, New York, 1989, pp. 116.

Chapter Fifteen

None

Chapter Sixteen

1. NASB-Daniel 10:13.
2. Frost, David: Interview with Billy Graham, Public television (PBS) 31 January 1993, Seattle area.
3. Fowler, Raymond E.: The Watchers: Bantam Books: New York, 1990 pp. 200.
4. NASB Matthew 7:15-21.
5. Fowler, Raymond E.: The Watchers: Bantam Books: New York, 1990 pp. 144-146.
6. NASB Matthew 22:30.
7. NASB 1Corinthians 2:9.
8. Cooper, William: Behold a Pale Horse: Light Technology Publishing, Sedonia Arizona 1991 pp. 70.

References

Alexander, Ben: Out From Darkness: College Publishing Co. Joplin, 1985.

Alnor, William M.: UFOs in the NEW AGE: Baker Book House, Grand Rapids 1992.

Blum, Howard: Out There: Pocket Star Books: New York 1990.

Bosveld, Jane: (1994, October) Cathedral Dreams. Omni.

Braden, Greg: Awakening to Zero Point: Sacred Spaces: Ann Arbor 1994.

Brooke, Tal: When the World Will be as One: Harvest House, Eugene 1989.

Cooper, William: Behold a Pale Horse: Light Technology Publishing, Sedona Arizona 1991.

Cumbey, Constance E.: The Hidden Dangers of the Rainbow: Huntington House, Shreveport 1983.

DK DIRECT LIMITED: UFO: The Continuing Enigma, Readers Digest, New York 1991.

Dobson, James C./Bauer, Garyl.: Children at Risk: Word Publishers, Dallas 1990.

Fiore, Edith: Encounters: Ballantine Books, New York 1989.

Fowler, Raymond E.: The Watchers: Bantam Books, New York 1991.

Freedenthal, Stacy. "Calling UFOs: Parking Availiable, no waiting." Tacoma New Tribune 26 Dec., 1992, reprinted from Dallas Morning News.

Frost, David: Interview with Billy Graham, Public Broadcasting (PBS) 31 January 1993.

Good, Timothy: Above Top Secret: Quill William Morrow: New York 1988.

Kelly, Christina. "Port Angeles Witch defies image, see herself as healer and helper": Tacoma News Tribune 28 Aug., 1995.

Lindemann, Michael: UFOs and the Alien Presence Six Viewpoints: 2020 Group Santa Barbra 1991.

McClain, Shirley: "Out On a Limb"-movie

McDermott, Terry, "For psychiatrist John Mack, "Abduction" is an alien matter, Seattle Times 1995.

Martin, Walter M.A. Phd.: The Kingdome of The Cults: Bethany House Publications, Minneapolis 1965.

Marrs, Texe: Mystery Mark of the New Age: Crossway Books, Westchester 1988.

Michaelsen, Johanna: The Beautiful Side of Evil: Harvest House, Eugene 1982.

NASB, All Biblical references are from the New American Standard Bible unless otherwise stated.

"Playing God" at the National institutes of Health, Our Sunday Visitor 30, Oct., 1994.

Randle, Kevin D. & Schmitt, Donald R.: UFO Crash at Roswell: New York 1991.

Redford, James: The Celestine Prophecy: Time Warner Co., New York, 1994.

Roberts, C. R., "Mount Rainier-Area Youth has Close Encounter in the Foothills, "Tacoma News Tribune": 24 April 1994.

Rawlings Maurice S. M.S.: To Hell and Back: Thomas Nelson Publishers: Nashville 1993.

Spangler, David/Thomson, William Irwin: Reimagination of the World, Bear and Co. Inc.: Santa Fe 1991.

Steiger, Brad, and Sherry Hansen: The Rainbow Conspiracy: Pinnacle Books-Windsor publishing Corp. New York 1994.

Strieber, Whitley: Communion: Avon Books, New York 1987.

Strieber, Whitley: Transformation: Avon Books, New york 1988.

Strieber, Whitley: Majestic: G.P. Putnam's Sons, New York 1989.

"The Alien Abduction Syndrome," After Dark Newsletter (Dreamland Report) Oct. 1995.

"The Lucifer Connection": Videocassette. John Anderson. 1990. VHS. 60 min.

"UFO Mysteries Solved in Bible." Sun, May, 1994.

"Vatican Telescope": Tacoma News Tribune: Dec 19., 1992.

Voice Network International: Over My Dead Body: Arlington Heights 1989.

Walters Ed.,/Francis: Gulf Breeze Sightings: Avon Books, New York 1991.

Websters's ll New Riverside Dictionary: Berkley Books, New York, 1984.

Glossary of Terms

ACLU - American Civil Liberties Union.

Agape Love - Unselfish love. A love that is Godly. Seeks the good in the other person.

Animal Mutilations - Mutilated carcasses of cattle found mostly in southwestern states. Cause of the mutilations are unknown but have a strong UFO connection. Advanced surgical and laser type surgery is used to remove the blood and critical organs of the animal leaving only the skin and bones.

Aquarian Age - Comes from the word Aquarius, the eleventh sign of the Zodiac. The Aquarian age, (often referred to by the hippies of the sixties peace and love era) also refers to the celestial sign that will bring man into a greater spiritual awareness.

Ascended Masters - Other christs or Gurus (spiritual leaders) that will appear to lead man into the New World Order.

Astral Projection - A psychic/spiritual method of leaving the body behind and traveling through space and or other dimensions.

Automatic Writing - Writing that is guided by an ungodly spiritual power.

Baba Muktannanda - A guru who initiates his followers with a supernatural force.

Boondoggle - A planned happening that turns into a complete mess.

Chanting - Saying specific words over and over as a hypnotic prayer. A far eastern religious practice.

Crop Circles - Geometric designs and circles found in flattened but not damaged wheat, corn and other grain fields across Europe and North America. Often appears overnight in geometric designs.

Demonic Mantras - Saying repetitious words that summon demon or evil beings. Related to chanting.

Dis-information - Information that is meant to confuse the facts. False information.

Eastern Mysticism - Spiritualism based on religions of the far east like Hinduism and Buddhism.

Exterrestrial Beings - Beings from an origin other than earth. Like belonging to UFOs. They are described in many different colors and shapes. Some tall, thin and transparent, some short and gray and still others human like.

Grays - Aliens who are often described by abductees as short extremely ugly and Gray in color.

Guru - Another name for a Hindu spiritual leader. Modern application of this term is used for most New Age spiritual teachers and leaders.

Hauntings - Movies and videos the portray scary spiritual episodes such as possession and evil spirit beings.

Hierarchy - Refers to a body of entities arranged in authoritive rank for rule purposes.

Hierophant - This term is derived from the Greek word hierophantes and is referred to as the person who is an interpreter of sacred and ancient mysteries.

Holistic Medicine - Medicine that is based on mind over matter. Does not rely on drugs but uses herbs and natural treatments for healing.

HMO - Health Maintenance Organization.

Humanism - A philosophy that deals with human achievements and interests. It is idealism concerning humans and what they can physically accomplish rather than dealing with abstract thoughts like religion.

Initiate - A person who has been initiated into an organization or society.

Inner Healing - Healing that deals with the inner man. Usually from hurts experienced from others. This term is used in both New Age and Christian circles.

Inner Transformation - A spiritual experience that changes how a person feels about themselves and toward others. This can be either a Godly experience or an ungodly experience.

Karma - Buddhism and Hinduism belief that one's conduct determines their future life.

Kingdom of Souls - Term not completely understood. It appears to be a spiritual place where New Agers hope to gather with the Luciferic Initiates.

Luciferic - Derived from Lucifer. As belonging to Lucifer or under his control or influence.

Luciferic Initiation - A term that describes an initiation into Lucifer's service.

Martial Arts - Oriental arts of self defense.

Maitreya - A name for the person often referred as the lord Maitreya. This person is supposed to represent the appearance of another christ.

Mass Initiations - A large group of people who have been initiated into an organization. In this case it represents a large number of people initiated into Lucifer's camp.

Metaphysical - Has a wide range of meaning. From a New Age perspective, it usually deals with supernatural events and reasoning which is abstract.

Meditation Exercises - A spiritual technique that trains the mind to concentrate on a specific subject, as in Yoga. It is a Hindu technique that allows the mind to enter another consciousness. A New Age term that describes a new social, economic and religious order for man.

Occultic Experiences - Channeling, witchcraft, seances, ESP. etc..

Other christs - A New Age belief that other christs or ascended masters will appear showing the way to a better life. They are anti-christs.

Parapsychology - A study of physic events (such as telepathy) that are beyond natural laws.

Phase Shifted - Signifies polarized energy flows. In this case it denotes a difference or shift in energy flow-one from another.

Planetary Culture - A New Age term that speaks of a utopian culture for earth.

Planetary Hierarchy - Human agents of the Luciferic Initiation who carry out the evolutionary plan designed by Satan.

Psychic Healing - Healing channeled through a human under control of ungodly spiritual guide or power.

Reincarnation - A belief where a person comes back after death in another form or body.

Remote Viewer - A term coined by the CIA. Refers to military personnel who were trained to use latent power of the soul in psychic experiments. Related to astral projection type exercises.

Resonating Field - A term that refers to an electrical energy cyclical vibration. Measured in cycles per second.

Sanat Kumara or - Another name for Satan. Also Shamballa referred to as lord of the world.

Shakti-pat - Is a force that is experienced by those who come under the influence of Baba Muktannanda.

Shamanism - Is a practice of summoning spirits. The practice goes back to Native primitive spiritualism.

Spiritual consciousness - This New Age term is used to explain a type of spiritual awareness. It deals with paranormal events like channeling and higher levels of consciousness.

Situational Ethics - A combination of circumstances and situations where solutions for any given moment are dependant on relativism. There are no moral absolutes. This term is related to Values clarification.

Trans-dimensional - Able to travel from one dimension to another dimension.

Universal Love - A New Age or Acquarian ideal that refers to a universal love for all mankind. It was practiced by the Hippies in the sixties and seventies as love and peace without morals.

Values Clarification - A nebulous method used to teach values in such a way as to make them valid only for the other person. Commonly used to explain away traditional values.

Virtual Reality - A computer generated simulation of reality.

Yoga - A Hindu philosophy that teaches control of the body through mind disciplines.

To order additional copies of

Lying Wonders
Evil Encounters of a Close Kind

please send $8.95
plus $1.75 shipping and handling to:

BOOKMARK
PO Box 1463
Milton, WA 98354

Continuing Research

You are invited to participate in an on-going research project concerning spiritual experiences; especially experiences concerning visions, apparitions, UFOs, and abductions you may have had. Your experiences (Godly or otherwise) are solicited for the purpose of continued research by the author. Your information will be held in confidence. No one to my knowledge has undertaken a project like this for the Christian body or for Christian research purposes.

If you have had a spiritual experience that you would like to share, please send your name, complete address, phone number and your story to:

BOOKMARK
PO Box 1463
Milton, WA 98354